DECOLONIZE
MULTICULTURALISM

ANTHONY C.
ALESSANDRINI

OR Books

New York · London

The *Decolonize That!* series is produced by OR Books in collaboration with *Warscapes* magazine.

© 2023 Anthony C. Alessandrini

Published by OR Books, New York and London
Visit our website at www.orbooks.com

All rights information: rights@orbooks.com

First printing 2023

Cataloging-in-Publication data is available from the Library of Congress. A catalog record for this book is available from the British Library.

Typeset by Lapiz Digital Services.

paperback ISBN 978-1-68219-353-2 • ebook ISBN 978-1-68219-354-9

DECOLONIZE
MULTICULTURALISM

Forthcoming in the *Decolonize That!* series

Decolonize Drag by Kareem Khubchandani

CONTENTS

EDITOR'S PREFACE

For the longest time, I thought it was nothing but a gory coincidence that I personally witnessed the second plane crash into the World Trade Center during my first week of graduate school at the City University of New York (CUNY). I was living in New York City, I happened to be downtown, wrong place at the wrong time. But I know now that it was more than that. The day's events marked the moment when the already troubled American university took an even darker turn, and which also transformed my personal trajectory. The entire span of my doctoral studies, most of the 2000s, was simultaneously about protesting the wars in Iraq and Afghanistan alongside a vocal core of graduate students and watching in horror as universities across the United States became openly complicit in American imperialism and neocon terror worldwide.

It was a confusing time for me. I had to reconcile being perceived as the enemy (a brown woman, probably Muslim even though I'm not) with also doubling up as the face of diversity and multiculturalism when it suited the university's purposes. As a doctoral student in a conservative literature program, I was pushed to submit to a canonical European tradition, while as an adjunct lecturer in the CUNY system, I was teaching postcolonial literature, literary theory and surveys of multicultural literature. So when Anthony Alessandrini asks, in *Decolonize Multiculturalism,* "What was I doing teaching the work of radical anti-colonial writers like Frantz Fanon, Mahasweta Devi, Jamaica Kincaid, and Ngũgĩ wa Thiong'o in that context? Was I contributing to decolonizing the university, or was I just helping management check off a box?" he speaks for many of us who have not always been able to articulate these predicaments.

I once believed that these antithetical forces only applied to literature programs in the US, which can be almost colonial in their approach to the major. Across the board, English literature majors are pushed to prioritize the British and American canon, and departments privilege a sort of ubiquitous "white lit" whose authors are presented as classics we must become marinated in. These curricula are supplemented by a sprinkling of "diversity" courses which can include Black and brown writers, women and queer writers, and sometimes, Irish writers. Comparative literature, English's multilingual cousin, has tended to be proudly European, and Romance languages comprise a majority of the foreign language study. As a student at the undergraduate or graduate level, literature programs can be intimidating. On the one hand, students are brainwashed into believing that reading, thinking and writing critically is the pinnacle of human excellence, whereas jobs and vocational training are sort of embarrassing business. And on the other hand, the rebel who may be wanting to step outside the designated parameters of the programs must collude with a fortress-like formation of requirements, electives, tracks and registration policies. Thus, it wasn't until I was properly employed at a university and became privy to the inner workings, the administrative conversations and the money flows, that I realized that there is a profound structural problem in American higher education.

And honestly, it wasn't until *Decolonize Multiculturalism* landed on my desk that I grasped the full story; a story that gets to the heart of the many departmental quarrels I have played in a part in (and always lost) since that fateful walk on Broadway when I saw the towers crumble into a heap.

The title of our series "Decolonize That! Handbooks for the Revolutionary Overthrow of Embedded Colonial Ideas," is avowedly playful and tongue-in-cheek; but Tony's *Decolonize Multiculturalism* is perhaps the most apt and serious iteration of the anchoring ideas of the project. Education is, without doubt, an active site of colonial practices and ideologies. Ngũgĩ wa Thiong'o famously described colonialism as "the night of the sword and the bullet" that is "followed by the morning of the chalk and the blackboard." Ngũgĩ was referring to the "civilizing" education and cultural missions that followed conquests but there should be no delusion that such programs were ever benign or peaceful. In particular, schools and universities have been places where the sword, the bullet, the chalk and the blackboard have worked in sync with one another, and the settler colonial United States remains the most drastic manifestation of these extremist approaches to education.

But this is not a book about universities or education per se so much as one supposedly progressive node within them: multiculturalism.

Today, in 2022, we have, once again, entered an era of student discontent across the planet and calls for universities to reform, repair and transform have become rampant. We're limping through a cataclysmic global pandemic with neither healing nor repair in sight. In the US, universities appear to have collectively pounced upon a fast fix. Hire more diverse faculty (though the *mot du jour* is really BIPOC) and develop all manner of anti-racism initiatives. The last few years have seen an unprecedented number of job openings for scholars of color and positions for deans and provosts of diversity and equity have multiplied. The plan is clear: BIPOC faculty teach diverse books and ideas, foster plurality, anti-racism and respect for pronouns, and usher in a better world for all. Sounds pretty fabulous, doesn't it?

Alas, this simple math born out of the liberal outrage against the Trump era has not exactly worked out. Between rising levels of police violence, renewed attacks on Critical Race Theory and abortion rights, and a pandemic-induced mental health crisis among students and educators, we seem worse for the wear despite the transformation efforts in American universities.

As we take stock of this messy situation, Tony's book is exactly what the doctor ordered for a variety of reasons. Indeed, much it is personal to me since CUNY was not only my first real experience of a public American university but it also provided me with a unique vantage point for understanding how the post-9/11 era and the "War on Terror" were sustained by universities generally. The book engages the term "multiculturalism" rather than "diversity." This makes sense since diversity has been co-opted by corporate entities and institutions to the point of becoming quite defanged. He explains that while university administrators tend to lump the two terms together, there is indeed a difference. Diversity emphasizes and respects differences while multiculturalism emphasizes inclusivity and group identity through which new futures can be conceived.

Most importantly, it is multiculturalism's brush with radical histories of the sixties and seventies that becomes a pivotal piece in this book, since it reminds us that the anti-racist and internationalist student movement at the time were working alongside and were shaped by decolonization struggles worldwide. As two-thirds of the planet shook off the yoke of colonialism and universities were stirring with discontent and uprisings, multiculturalism (in its flawed form) was born. Yet, as Tony readily admits, while everyone agrees that multiculturalism is important and desired, neither the left nor the right really like it. For the left, in particular, it is just a corporate catchword. In these circumstances, Tony assigns himself a truly difficult task: to convince the readers that "hidden inside the flabbiest, most compromised, most hypocritical forms of multiculturalism today are the traces of radical struggles, mostly those of students and other young people, who fought (and are still fighting) to change the order of the world in the name of anti-racism, anti-capitalism, feminism, queer liberation, and internationalism—that is to say, in the name of a true decolonization." And you know what I am going to say next (I'm the editor of this series, after all): He succeeds valiantly.

From the Reagan to the Trump era, from the canon/ culture wars of the eighties to the relentless police violence on campuses by way of a heavily surveilled student polity continually protesting for change, *Decolonize Multiculturalism* takes the readers on a dizzying journey through the rotten structures of imperial violence that support educational institutions. It shows that our sparkling and woke new universities—replete with diversity centers, diversity provosts and Rainbow centers—are only evidence that things have not quite gone right.

But there is hope, there is always beautiful and radical hope. Our hero, Angela Davis, says that "sometimes we have to do the work even though we don't yet see a glimmer on the horizon that it's actually going to be possible." *Decolonize Multiculturalism* is that precise glimmer. From that fateful day I walked up that New York City avenue and saw the towers fall, a new energetic era of communication, analyses, protests, discontents and revolutions has dawned. Tony offers the roadmap for us to understand this moment and inspires us to join the fight. Somewhere within that, he even does a bit of decolonizing.

Bhakti Shringarpure

July 2022

Introduction

DREAMS BEGIN HERE

Once upon a time, in the last year of the twentieth century, I got my first full-time teaching job. It was at Kent State University, a public university in northeastern Ohio, about halfway between Cleveland and Akron. If you're a little fuzzy on your Ohio geography (I sure was at the time), that's right about where the famously polluted Cuyahoga River once caught fire—or, if you prefer, about equidistant between the birthplaces of LeBron James and Judith Butler. I was fresh out of grad school, with a newly minted PhD in Literatures in English from Rutgers University. I had spent the past decade studying and engaging with literary and theoretical approaches that came directly out of the radical political struggles of those who had gone before: postcolonial studies, critical race theory, cultural studies, and feminist and queer theory. I went out into the world as a true believer, ready to share these radical visions with a new generation of students. At Kent State, I was hired to be the English department's first "postcolonialist." Ready to rise to the occasion, I enthusiastically put together an undergraduate course in postcolonial literature—the first such course ever to be offered at the university.

It was a big hit with the powers that be. Indeed, I was told by an enthusiastic administrator that the class would immediately be added to the list of courses students could take to fulfill their "diversity requirement." The fact that there even was such a thing was news to me. You can still find a description of that "diversity requirement" on the Kent State website: its stated purpose was and is "to help educate students to live in a world of diverse communities, many of which are becoming increasingly permeated with cultural and ideological differences." Aside from the administrative word salad of that last phrase (permeated?), what made that sort of language jarring when I first encountered it was my own experience of having moved to Northeastern Ohio from Brooklyn; it was, as far as I could tell, very much not "a world of diverse communities." Soon after moving, I found myself haunted by a feeling that something very particular was missing from the texture of my everyday life, although I couldn't put my finger on it. A few weeks in, it came to me with a jolt: it was the first place I had lived where the only language I ever overheard in stores or in the street or on campus was English.

Weirder still was the imbalance between the stated importance of this "diversity requirement" and the relatively little institutional space it took up at the university. For the weighty task of "educating students to live in a world of diverse communities," it appeared, a total of two courses would suffice: one addressing "domestic (US) issues" and one addressing "global issues." My postcolonial lit class would fall into the baggy category of "global issues," alongside courses like Introduction to Archaeology, The Roman Achievement, European Politics, and Introduction to Ethics.

We'll be encountering the logic of the diversity requirement, a cornerstone of "multiculturalism" in today's colleges and universities, in a lot more detail later in this book. But back then I was still a tender beginner, so this diversity requirement thing was news to me. Excited as I was about teaching a class on postcolonial literature, and relieved as I was to have it on the books, there was something sickening about this notion of "diversity" as a requirement that needed to be forced upon students, albeit in small, measured quantities, like a vitamin supplement. Apparently, it was something that the university considered to be external to students' lives, separate from and unrelated to their own experiences or identities. There was this undifferentiated category of *students*, and then there was this world of "diverse communities" that they would have to be taught how to live in (but didn't any of them *come from* these communities in the first place?). Ergo, there was this thing called "diversity" to be added to students' educational diet. Diversity requirement classes clearly fell into the "eat it, it's good for you" category for college administrators.

What was I doing teaching the work of radical anti-colonial writers like Frantz Fanon, Mahasweta Devi, Jamaica Kincaid, and Ngũgĩ wa Thiong'o in that context? Was I contributing to decolonizing the university, or was I just helping management check off a box?

Diversity University, or the Longer You Stay the More You Pay

It's no exaggeration to say that those questions soon drove me, not just out of that job, but for a while, out of the profession of teaching altogether. Specifically, in the aftermath of the invasions and occupations of Afghanistan and Iraq, when the imperial wars of the US turned into literal colonization, it became impossible for me to imagine teaching *post*-colonialism to American students. I decided I needed to do more learning before I could do any more teaching, so I entered an MA program in Near Eastern Studies, intending to study Arabic and then—well, that was less clear, but at the time I would say things like "I would really like to do human rights work." Old academic friends and new activist friends all seemed to agree I was sort of nuts. "You know," a fellow student in the program confided as we were getting drunk at a reception after a lecture, "a lot of people think that you're with the FBI or CIA or something, because your story really doesn't check out." I was fortunate to be able to spend a couple of years moving through activist spaces—mostly in New York, but also in Cairo and Istanbul, and then for a few months in Palestine—that provided me with precious new ways of understanding what radical knowledge production could look like.[1]

But finally, coming up against the question of having to continue to eat and pay rent, I lucked into a job teaching English at Kingsborough Community College in Brooklyn. It's a two-year college, one of twenty-five campuses that make up the City University

1   One such radical knowledge production project I was honored to work on at the time was the World Tribunal on Iraq. For readers who aren't familiar with the work and legacy of the WTI—a grassroots project intended to help hold the perpetrators of the Iraq War accountable for their crimes— see the brilliant account provided by my WTI comrade Ayça Çubukçu in *For the Love of Humanity: The World Tribunal on Iraq* (Philadelphia: University of Pennsylvania Press, 2018).

of New York (CUNY), which is in turn the largest urban university in the world, serving more than a quarter of a million students from across the city and around the world.

CUNY is fond of touting itself as "diversity university." There's a good and valid reason for this: like the city it serves, the student body at CUNY is, by almost every measure, an ethnically and racially diverse community like few others in this country. In its recent advertising campaigns, the university's administration has gone all in on this narrative: diversity as a mission.

Needless to say, that's not the whole story. From the moment it was founded in 1847 as the Free Academy—which later became City College—CUNY was envisioned as a radical experiment in public education. As Dr. Horace Webster, the first president of the Free Academy, declared at its opening ceremony: "The experiment is to be tried, whether the children of the people, the children of the whole people, can be educated; and whether an institution of the highest grade, can be successfully controlled by the popular will, not by the privileged few" (it should probably be noted, however, that the actual founder of the Free Academy was Townsend Harris, a wealthy businessman and politico).[2] From the beginning, CUNY was tuition-free, thus seeming to live up to its mission of radical inclusiveness.

But CUNY was also, for more than a century, diversity-free: in other words, completely segregated. As late as 1969, CUNY's flagship campus, City College, located in the heart of Harlem, was 97 percent white. Brooklyn College was 96 percent white, despite the fact that more than a third of the borough's residents were Black or Hispanic. The subsequent desegregation of CUNY, which ushered in the diversity celebrated today by college administrators and enshrined in glossy ad campaigns, was in fact accomplished largely via the struggles of student movements.

In the spring of 1969, students at every CUNY campus rose up in protest; student activists occupied administrative buildings at Brooklyn College and Queens College, and a student strike shut down City College for two weeks. Student organizers, together with a handful of faculty and staff supporters, faced

2   See Michelle Ronda, "The Children of the Whole People Can Be Educated," in *Women on the Role of Public Higher Education: Personal Reflections from CUNY's Graduate Center*, ed. Deborah S. Gambs and Rose M. Kim (New York: Palgrave Macmillan, 2015), p. 29.

down institutional sanctions, police violence, attacks by racist right-wing thugs, and the hostility of "law and order" city politicians who called for even more violence to be brought against "disruptive" students—not to mention university administrators more ready to call in the cops than to address student demands.

These student movements—from the Third World Coalition at Hunter College, to the Black and Puerto Rican Student Community and the W. E. B. Du Bois Club at City College, to the Black League of Afro-American Collegians and the Puerto Rican Alliance at Brooklyn College, to the various chapters of Students for a Democratic Society that were active at campuses throughout the CUNY system—were deeply influenced and inspired by ongoing struggles for decolonization, which they linked to their anti-racist work within the university. As one student activist writes in his account of the history of struggle at CUNY: "The rapid decolonization of Africa, the Cuban Revolution and the appearance of armed national liberation movements across Latin America, the upheavals taking place in China, and the heroic resistance of the Vietnamese to the aggression of the mightiest military power in human history all contributed to a situation in which oppressed people everywhere imagined that they could make great gains through struggle." Today's CUNY, the diversity university, wouldn't exist without these struggles to decolonize the "people's university."[3]

The desegregation of CUNY has rightly been called "the most significant civil rights victory in higher education in the history of the United States."[4] Thanks to gains won by student protesters—most prominently, a new open admissions policy—the demographics of the

3   For excellent accounts, see Christopher Gunderson, "The Struggle for CUNY: A History of the CUNY Student Movement, 1969-1999" (available online); Martha Biondi, "'Brooklyn College Belongs to Us': Black Students and the Transformation of Public Higher Education in New York City," in Clarence Thomas, ed., *Civil Rights in New York City* (New York: Fordham University Press, 2011); Bhargav Rani, "Revolution and CUNY: Remembering the 1969 Fight for Open Admissions," *GC Advocate* (30 July 2018); Tahir H. Butt, "'You Are Running a de Facto Segregated University': Racial Segregation and the City University of New York, 1961-1968," in *The Strange Careers of the Jim Crow North: Segregation and Struggle outside of the South*, ed. Brian Purnell and Jeanne Theoharis in collaboration with Komozi Woodard (New York: New York University Press, 2019); and Salvatore Asaro, "Campus Unrest Part I: Queens College in the Spring of 1969" (November 5, 2018, available online), as well as the still-active and very awesome "CUNY Struggle" blog.

4   Biondi, "'Brooklyn College Belongs to Us,'" p. 161.

university shifted radically. The number of Black and Puerto Rican students attending CUNY increased by more than 170 percent in just three years; at the same time, enrollment of white students increased as well. Overall, enrollment for first-time students at CUNY nearly doubled between 1969 and 1972. But these gains were followed almost immediately by the systematic defunding of the university by city, state, and federal governments, at a time when white flight from the city led to the defunding of almost all public services in New York City. Beginning in 1975—after being tuition-free for more than 125 years—CUNY began charging tuition. It took its toll almost immediately: by the end of the 1970s, there was a decline of over 62,000 students in enrollment, with a 50 percent decline in the number of Black and Latino students in the entering class of 1980.

And tuition keeps going up, increasing more than 30 percent between 2010 and 2020. That's because state and city funding for CUNY, and for public education more generally, keeps going down: the share of the university's budget that comes from tuition has risen from 20 percent to nearly 50 percent since 1990. I'll let Juvanie Piquant, former chair of the CUNY Student Senate and a leader of the CUNY Rising Alliance that's fighting to make CUNY free again, sum it up: "All the things that were good enough for the white working class became too good for the diverse working class that emerged in New York in the second half of the twentieth century."[5]

To sum up: we have here the story of a public university that was originally economically accessible, but racially segregated. Today, it is (officially) racially desegregated, but largely economically inaccessible (i.e. it is segregated by other means). Remember this formula: we're going to encounter it again on our journey towards understanding "multiculturalism" as it has come to be experienced via the economic austerity imposed by neoliberalism.

The most accurate representation of CUNY's current relationship to its diverse student body might be seen in another slick advertising campaign. The "15 to Finish" campaign pushes students to take 15 credits per semester and 30 per year. "Do the math," scolds a series of ads that are everywhere on campus (especially at the two-year colleges), aimed at a population of students almost all of whom work full-time and many of whom have families. Most of the ads feature students of color. I mean, "think, dream, do" for sure, but hurry up, because the longer you stay, the more you pay.

5   Juvanie Piquant, "Imposing Tuition at CUNY Was Systemic Racism. This Year, We Can Fix It," *Gotham Gazette* (March 26, 2021).

Dreams Begin Here

Kingsborough Community College, where I've taught since 2005, is a poor stepchild even within the increasingly impoverished CUNY system as a whole. The story of Kingsborough embodies many of the contradictions of the larger story of CUNY. For one thing, the decision to establish a community college in Brooklyn in the early 1960s came at least in part as a response to grassroots demands from community groups, largely representing communities of color, including young activists who were fighting for access to a CUNY education. By 1964, when the logistics of establishing Kingsborough were being worked out, local community leaders called for the college to be built in the largely Black neighborhood of Bedford-Stuyvesant— one of the many communities whose residents had been largely shut out of CUNY. Responding to this suggestion at a contentious community meeting, Brooklyn College Dean Abraham Goodhartz snorted: "Why send students to areas of degradation and blight?"[6] The message was clear:

6   See "Forces Fight Dawn-Dusk Battle for New College," *New York Amsterdam News* (March 7, 1964); the story is recounted with vigor in Michael Woodsworth, *Battle for Bed-Stuy: The Long War on Poverty in New York City* (Cambridge: Harvard University Press, 2016), p. 285-86. Endless thanks to my Kingsborough colleague Libby Garland (who, unlike me, is an actual historian) for finding and sharing a wealth of primary documents related to the founding of the college.

"CUNY students" and "people who live in Bedford-Stuyvesant" were, in the eyes of those like Dean Goodhartz (Charles Dickens couldn't have invented a better name for such a perfidious character), mutually exclusive categories that should never be allowed to overlap.

Thanks to interventions by local politicians and CUNY administrators, Kingsborough was instead built in the hyper-segregated white neighborhood of Manhattan Beach, on the site of a former Merchant Marines training ground (the World War II era "temporary" barracks are still used to house classrooms), where it remains today. It'll take you an hour to get there on the train or bus from Bed-Stuy, on a good day. It's actually a lot quicker and easier to get to Kingsborough from the largely white enclaves of Staten Island or Long Island, where many of the college's white faculty and administrators live, as long as you have a car (and they do). But nevertheless, our College Diversity Statement declares: "The administration, faculty, staff, and students at Kingsborough Community College believe that the college is best served by having a campus that is truly diverse." And if you don't believe the diversity statement, come visit the campus: right there at the front gate, sandwiched between the security "checkpoint" manned by armed campus police (where students are often forced to line up for the "100% ID check" that will probably make them late for class) and the stretch of sidewalk that's usually occupied by uniformed military recruiters making their bloody pitch to students entering and leaving campus, you'll find a glossy poster advertising Kingsborough's commitment to diversity.

And in spite of its unwelcoming location, by most measures, Kingsborough, like community colleges throughout the United States, really does serve a diverse population of students. Nearly 70 percent of Kingsborough students fall into the category of minority students (the official institutional categories include Black, Hispanic, Asian, and Native American students). More than half of Kingsborough's students were born outside the US, representing 142 different countries and 73 different native languages. Sixty percent of Kingsborough students are the first generation in their families to attend college. Most of them have come of age in the era of austerity, which means some other statistics are in order: roughly 48 percent of CUNY students suffer from food insecurity, 55 percent of CUNY students suffer from housing insecurity, and nearly 15 percent of CUNY students are or have been homeless while attending college.[7]

7   Ben Chapman, "Thousands of CUNY Students Experience Homelessness and Food Insecurity, Report Says," *New York Daily News* (27 March 2019).

This has a stark effect: a 2017 study showed that 75 percent of those who dropped out of Kingsborough had a financial "red flag" in their accounts, due to owing money or losing their funding.[8] When I was first teaching there, I would occasionally find a form in my mailbox with one of my student's names on it. In the most brutal bureaucratese, it would inform me that the student was on the "purge list" because they owed the college money and that I should forbid them from attending class until they cleared up their financial red flag. (Reader, I never did.)

That particular draconian practice has stopped, but the college still has ways of making students pay up or get out. A few years ago, I was part of a meeting called in response to student demands that the college do more to support undocumented students (this was not long after the election of Donald Trump). One student pointed out that many undocumented students were forced to leave school because the college refused to allow them to pay their tuition in installments. To be eligible for the installment plan, a student needed either a bank account or a credit card, and either one of these

8   Andrew Gounardes and Timothy Hunter, "The Right to a Free and Quality Higher Education in New York," *Gotham Gazette* (November 26, 2019).

was impossible to get without a social security number. Undocumented students who couldn't pay their whole tuition up front in cash—a significant amount of money for those attending full-time—were thus being purged from the college. After a bit of hemming and hawing, a vice-president, whose lousy suit belied the fact that he made a tidy six-figure salary, declared matter-of-factly: "Well, it might be that some people just aren't financially prepared to attend college." This was right around the time that our community college's administration announced our new motto: "Kingsborough: Dreams Begin Here."

Chapter One

STARTING FROM WHERE WE ARE, OR DECOLONIZATION ISN'T JUST FOR T-SHIRTS!

So far, I've mostly been telling my own story. But within it lie the larger stories that will drive this book. First, there are the struggles of anti-racist and internationalist student movements who took their cue from ongoing struggles for decolonization and fought to decolonize their universities in the 1960s and 1970s. Next, there's the violent suppression of these movements: not just the overt violence of the police, but also the more covert violence of neoliberal policies of austerity unleashed against these movements. Finally, there's the condition of educational austerity that prevails today, where the gauzy promise of "dreams begin here" quickly gives way to the steely logic that lies beneath: "the longer you stay the more you pay."

Although it may not be immediately obvious, each of these stories is integral to the rise of multiculturalism—that is, the form of multiculturalism that has dominated universities and other institutions, which I'll be calling "institutional multiculturalism." Without the demands made by student movements fighting to desegregate, democratize, and ultimately decolonize colleges and universities, the institutional strategy of multiculturalism as a form of "diversity management" wouldn't have had to be invented. This sort of multiculturalism, as it starts to become established in the 1970s, nicely fits the emergent purposes of neoliberalism. That same velvet glove then serves the additional purpose of covering the iron fist of the militarized campus established by legislators and university administrators in the 1970s and 1980s (just as neoliberalism is getting started in earnest). And finally, what I call "austerity multiculturalism" is the guiding ideology of universities—especially public universities—today. The "diversity requirement" that I first learned about at Kent State is a perfect example of the ethos of austerity multiculturalism: do more with less—in this case, do a lifetime of "diversity work" with just two three-credit classes!

From Rutgers to Kent State to CUNY, I've spent the past twenty-five or so years teaching at public institutions. This has given me plenty of experience stuck in the frustrating, unproductive muck surrounding institutional multiculturalism. On my best days, I still see myself as a politicized teacher and scholar, and even an occasional activist. Like others who share this territory, my intellectual work is grounded in approaches that come out of histories of political struggle, including the struggle for decolonization. But depoliticized versions of these radical intellectual traditions have been gradually absorbed into the "multicultural" curriculum of the neoliberal university.

How did we get here?

A Word on Winning

The book you're reading is far from being a complete history of how we got to this point; many others have already done this work, and I've merely attempted to build upon some of their insights to sharpen my polemic. You'll find these other works discussed throughout, with a full list of sources for further reading (and doing) at the end. But you won't find a detailed definition of "multiculturalism" here, or a discussion of the various theoretical and analytic debates around what the term means. In calling us to our task—decolonization—I'm less interested in what multiculturalism *is* (and, as we'll see, no one can quite agree on a single definition anyway) than in what it *does*.

As the title suggests, this book is a call for a collective transformation of multiculturalism as it currently functions in order to reclaim it as a weapon in the struggle for decolonization. That means going beyond simply criticizing multiculturalism for what it currently does or fails to do—although we'll have to spend some time surveying the wreckage. Instead, I'll ask us to attend to the longer-term effort needed to recapture the radical legacy of multiculturalism's suppressed history and to imagine how this radical energy can be unleashed for the political struggles of the present and the future. I am therefore deeply indebted to, and will try to build upon and contribute to, the kind of transformative work that scholar-activists like Ruth Wilson Gilmore summon us to with her call to reimagine multicultural studies as "Liberation Studies."[1]

It's therefore necessary to say a few words about *decolonization*. Like other authors in the "Decolonize That!" series, I'm highly aware that "decolonize!" can become little more than a t-shirt slogan. Literally: have a look on Etsy and you'll find plenty of options—and lots of handmade decolonization tote bags too. Actually, as I was writing this chapter on my laptop, sitting outside a coffee shop in Brooklyn, somebody walked by wearing a t-shirt that said: "Decolonize Your Bookshelf." (I mean, it's Brooklyn, so it's not that much of a coincidence.)[2]

1   See Afua Cooper, Rinaldo Walcott and Lekeisha Hughes, "Robin D. G. Kelley and Fred Moten in Conversation," *Critical Ethnic Studies* 4.1 (2018), p. 157.

2   If you enjoyed that joke, then you probably need to read the book that kicked off this "Decolonize That!" series:

This ever-present, very real threat of co-optation means that our work needs to be unsparing.

But being unsparing—as I'll try to be in the pages to come—is not the same as becoming what Michel Foucault called "the sad militant": "Do not think that one has to be sad in order to be militant," Foucault insists, "even though the thing one is fighting is abominable."[3] The fight I'm proposing is deadly serious, but we can still be happy warriors.

The establishment of today's institutional version of "multiculturalism" is largely a story of the counterrevolution against the social movements of the 1960s and 1970s, carried out by the state but also by corporations and university administrators. For a Gen-Xer like me who came of age politically in the Age of Reagan, radical politics has generally been about fighting for causes that seem destined always to lose. It's easy to start wearing those losses as battle scars, like medals of honor, to show off your political purity. Decolonization, on the

Grégory Pierrot's brilliant *Decolonize Hipsters* (New York: OR Books, 2020).

3   Michel Foucault, "Preface," in Gilles Deleuze and Felix Guattari, *Anti-Oedipus: Capitalism and Schizophrenia*, trans. Robert Hurley, Mark Seem, and Helen R. Land (Minneapolis: University of Minnesota Press, 1983), p. xli-xlii.

other hand, is about winning. That's why I think often of the warning given by one of my first and best teachers, Bruce Robbins, that we must not allow ourselves to "come to believe that any success in winning support is in itself a fatal sign of co-optation or evidence that the movement was not progressive to begin with." Even those decolonization t-shirts signal a crack in things; it's up to us to keep pushing until the current world breaks wide open. That means guarding against co-optation but also simultaneously allowing ourselves to imagine the struggle as being winnable. Gilmore sums it up in her exhortation to prison abolitionists: "Fight to win."[4]

An Agenda for Total Disorder

Decolonization is not a metaphor; let's begin there. Writing from within movements against settler colonialism, Eve Tuck and K. Wayne Yang provide a straightforward alternative to the metaphorical use of the term (like wearing "Decolonize X!" on a t-shirt): "Decolonization brings about the repatriation of Indigenous land and life; it is not a metaphor for other things we want to do to

4   Bruce Robbins, *Feeling Global: Internationalism in Distress* (New York: New York UP, 1999), p. 116-17; Ruth Wilson Gilmore, "The Worrying State of the Anti-Prison Movement," *Social Justice: A Journal of Crime, Conflict & World Order* (February 23, 2015).

improve our societies and schools." For Linda Tuhiwai Smith, a scholar of indigenous education and author of the book *Decolonizing Methodologies*, this means beginning by decolonizing our most basic methods of writing, teaching, and thinking. The very thing that we call "research," viewed "from the vantage point of the colonized, is inextricably linked to European imperialism and colonialism. The word itself, 'research,' is probably one of the dirtiest words in the indigenous world's vocabulary."[5]

The most straightforward definition of decolonization, which still provides a bottom line for those of us who want to work on decolonization as a *real* rather than metaphorical force, was provided at the beginning of the 1960s by Frantz Fanon in *The Wretched of the Earth*: "Decolonization, which sets out to change the order of the world, is clearly an agenda for total disorder." Of course, a political or educational project—not to mention a book—built around "an agenda for total disorder"

5   Eve Tuck and K. Wayne Yang, "Decolonization Is not a
     Metaphor," *Decolonization: Indigeneity, Education & Society* 1.1
     (2012), p. 1; Linda Tuhiwai Smith, *Decolonizing Methodologies:
     Research and Indigenous Peoples*, second edition (London:
     Zed Books, 2012), p. 1. Also see "Decolonizing Education:
     A Conversation with Linda Tuhiwai Smith," *Los Angeles Review
     of Books* (May 18, 2021).

sounds like a contradiction. But Tuhiwai Smith, who takes Fanon's words as a starting point, calls our attention to the fact that like "research," "order"—or at least our contemporary idea of it—is both a cause and a result of imperialism. This is the sort of "orderliness" that leads us to draw "common sense" connections between things we have been taught to see as both natural and also naturally related to each other, including "the nature of imperial social relations; the activities of Western science; the establishment of trade; the appropriation of sovereignty; the establishment of law."[6] To her list of "orderly" things, we might add the establishment of market capitalism, ethnic and racial hierarchies, compulsory heterosexuality, and binarized gender identity.

So from the perspective of the colonized, while the colonizers claimed (and still claim) to be the bringers of order, the truth is that imperialism and colonialism "brought complete disorder to colonized peoples, disconnecting them from their histories, their landscapes, their languages, their social relations and their own ways of thinking, feeling, and interacting with the world." Just as important, as Tuhiwai Smith reminds us, is the

6   Frantz Fanon, *The Wretched of the Earth*, trans. Richard Philcox (New York: Grove, 2004), p. 2; Tuhiwai Smith, *Decolonizing Methodologies*, p. 27.

extent to which this imperialist "order" still determines how our educational institutions function, even on the most basic level. Among the many other things that it was and is, colonization "was a process of systematic fragmentation which can still be seen in the disciplinary carve-up of the indigenous world: bones, mummies and skulls to the museums, art work to private collectors, languages to linguistics, 'customs' to anthropologists, beliefs and behaviors to psychologists" (and, I would add, stories and poetry to literature departments).[7] They don't call them "disciplines" for nothing; colonial violence remains at work even in the university's seemingly objective form of ordering itself along disciplinary lines.

It is *this* ever-present, still-powerful colonial order of the world that we have in mind when those of us working together on this collective series declare our desire to *Decolonize That!*

Any Decolonization Is a Success: Black Lives Matter

In order to try to answer the question I asked above— "How did we get here?"—we'll need to spend some time historicizing this thing we call "multiculturalism."

7   Tuhiwai Smith, *Decolonizing Methodologies*, p. 28.

This will also mean unpacking the connections and distinctions between multiculturalism and a term that often keeps it company in the mouths of university administrators and other corporate types: "diversity." I'll have much more to say about this in chapter three, but for now I'll just note that understanding their relationship also involves doing some historicizing. That is, "diversity" becomes the marker of institutional efforts to separate anti-racism from its roots in radical student movements, while "multiculturalism" does a similar sort of depoliticizing work with, and against, the powerful history of radical internationalism found within these same movements. Telling that story involves doing the hard and painful work of revisiting the many forms of violence unleashed upon these movements—by the state, by corporations, and by universities themselves.

Here's where I must insert a disclaimer: I'm not a historian. I didn't even take a US history class in college. Fortunately, I'm smart enough to hang around with historians and to read and learn from their work; I'll be drawing on the work of many who have mapped this history better than I ever could. But the historicizing work you'll find in this book is anyway more polemical than painstaking. I'm going to try to convince you that hidden inside the flabbiest, most compromised, most hypocritical forms of multiculturalism today are the traces of radical struggles, mostly those of students and other young people, who fought (and are still fighting) to change the order of the world in the name of anti-racism, anti-capitalism, feminism, queer liberation, and internationalism—that is to say, in the name of a true decolonization.

There's a revolutionary kernel secreted inside the bland exterior of today's institutional multiculturalism. The historical energy of a decolonized multiculturalism has the potential to crack that surface, like a weed breaking through the smoothly paved cement path that leads to the Multicultural Center; but it can't emerge without a lot of us showing up with sledgehammers.

So part of our mission is to bring that hidden history back to the surface. Decolonization is always a historical process, Fanon reminds us, because "it can only be understood, it can only find its significance and become self-coherent insofar as we can discern the history-making movement which gives it form and substance." Tuhiwai Smith agrees: from the perspective of indigenous politics, simply put, "there is unfinished business."[8] As I'll be repeating in one way or another

8   Fanon, *Wretched of the Earth*, p. 2; Tuhiwai Smith, *Decolonizing Methodologies*, p. 34.

throughout this book, decolonizing multiculturalism begins with the act of returning it to its radical roots.

That's hard work; you can't put it on a t-shirt. I'm inviting you to look at this thing we call *multiculturalism* with a new set of eyes, without falling back on all the stuff that we think we already know about it. If you're reading this book, you've probably already got some feelings about "multiculturalism." Me too. My teaching and research and writing are all informed by approaches that would likely be included in most definitions of "multiculturalism": postcolonial studies, Middle Eastern studies, feminist and gender studies, critical race studies, queer studies, disability studies, critical university studies. This book comes at least in part out of my experience, but it's not an objective account or an ethnography; it's an attempt to light a certain kind of fire.

I've already used the word "unsparing," a term I've always associated with the work of Frantz Fanon. The opening chapter of *The Wretched of the Earth*, a book published just days before his untimely death in 1961, is an immersion course in decolonization; he uses the word twelve times on the first three pages alone. But there's one seemingly simple sentence from those opening pages that I've been wrestling with for years. It comes just after Fanon has summed up the goals of decolonization by unexpectedly pulling out the famous New Testament verse: "The last shall be first." Decolonization, he continues, is simply "a verification of this." And then comes this sentence: "At a descriptive level, therefore, any decolonization is a success."[9]

It's a hell of a mic drop, but what does it mean? He lays that cryptic sentence on us, ends the section, and moves on. On the simplest level, I think Fanon is trying to point out the distinction between true decolonization and other, less ambitious movements, like achieving nominal political independence for the colony (or, in our terms, maybe pushing for the establishment of a Multicultural Center). Fanon had no time for such limited goals. Naming the struggle "decolonization" commits us to setting a course for a more transformative horizon—after all, it's the literal overturning of the world as we know it, "an agenda for total disorder." One reason for continuing to fight for decolonization today is that it has not yet happened.

But Fanon is also declaring the power of the descriptive level itself, in a way that's crucial for our work today. My thinking about this (and many other things) has been influenced and inspired most strongly by the Black Lives Matter movement. On the descriptive level, "Black lives matter" is a simple statement,

9   Fanon, *Wretched of the Earth*, p. 2.

but it contains and creates the most transformative of effects. What "Black lives matter" describes is of course not the actual state of things. In a society where Black people are killed by the state on a daily basis with complete impunity, Black lives are revealed not to "matter," in the most literal sense, day in and day out. Rather, "Black lives matter" describes an alternative reality that needs to be fought for and brought into existence through anti-racist struggle—in the largest sense, through decolonization.

It's important to add that Black Lives Matter is about so much more than that one declarative statement: it names a decentralized and non-hierarchical movement that has become the largest political movement in US history; the Movement for Black Lives has, among other things, issued a powerful and practical platform for racial and economic justice that has deeply influenced the thinking of a new generation of political activists and even some progressive office-holders; and beginning in the summer of 2020, BLM has inspired the greatest popular uprising against racialized state violence in the history of the United States, one that has spread far beyond its borders.

But think for a moment about the racist hysteria provoked by folks doing nothing more than just saying or chanting or tweeting out that simple, descriptive statement: "Black lives matter." Think of all the ink (and blood) spilled in the name of the defensive (racist) insistence that "all lives matter" and "blue lives matter" and on and on. White people—not just the police and their militia and vigilante and political helpers and enablers, but all those who support them—are literally willing to kill Black people (and anyone standing in solidarity with them) simply for asserting that three-word phrase.

We begin to get a sense of what Fanon means by the power of the descriptive level, and how it must contribute to the work of decolonization today. The work of bringing into existence a world in which Black lives truly matter remains to be done. But the statement "Black lives matter" has already in and of itself named the struggle, creating the "agenda for total disorder" that we need to follow. Transforming the statement "Black lives matter" from an aspiration or demand to a reality means changing the order of the world, on every level. The Black Feminist tradition has insisted upon this for years: as the Combahee River Collective put it back in 1977, "If Black women were free, it would mean that everyone else would have to be free since our freedom would necessitate the destruction of all systems of oppression"; or as Ruth Wilson Gilmore summed it up more recently, "when Black lives matter, everybody lives better."[10]

Sometimes, the most radical political work, even work directly focused on changing people's material reality, has to start with the work of description, or re-description. That seems like a strange statement to make after watching the streets light up with the popular uprisings against racist state violence across the United States. But if we're really to set an agenda for total disorder, then we need to be prepared to fight on all fronts, and to be clear about where we're setting our sights and what destination we have in our mind's eye. In presenting the current state of multiculturalism, and in attempting to call us to attend to its radical possibilities, I will be as unsparing as possible. That's the necessary first step for re-describing the world, which is to say re-imagining it, which is to say, transforming it. It's a matter of decolonizing the mind, in the words of the great Kenyan writer Ngũgĩ wa Thiong'o.

10   *The Combahee River Collective Statement: Black Feminist Organizing in the Seventies and Eighties* (Albany, NY: Kitchen Table: Women of Color Press, 1986); Keeanga-Yamahtta Taylor, "Black Feminism and the Combahee River Collective," *Monthly Review* (January 1, 2019); "Ruth Wilson Gilmore Makes the Case for Abolition," *Intercepted Podcast* (June 10, 2020).

About This Book

I realize that *unsparing* is not necessarily a synonym for *fun*. Be that as it may, I hope you enjoy reading this book. I've got, as they say, all the feels about this thing called multiculturalism as it exists today, and I hope that wherever you're coming from, you'll find something meaningful here.

In keeping with the goals of the "Decolonize That!" series, this book resists the idea that there is a difference between writing for an "academic" audience and for a "general" audience. There is no inside or outside to what has come to be called "the academy"; there is no "general" audience. There are only institutions, languages, and spaces that are more or less accessible, more or less fenced off, more or less jealously guarded, more or less expensive, more or less plastered over with warnings, more or less patrolled by cliques, more or less password-protected, more or less self-consciously intimidating, more or less violently policed, more or less dedicated to defining themselves variously as "intellectual," "down-to-earth," "resistant," "realistic," "accessible," "anti-elitist," "pragmatic," "popular"—name the catch-word, and you'll find, consciously or not, a scheme for keeping some of us in and some of us out.

Much of this book will focus on colleges and universities, and I would love it if some of its readers are students, since it is both a book about trying to recapture the energy of student movements of the past and one deeply inspired by the youth and student movements of today. But the work of the university isn't only relevant to those of us who study and work inside its walls. The work of the university is the concern of everyone, even if the neoliberal university's best trick is to try to convince much of the public that what goes on behind its high walls is none of their concern—or worse, simply beyond their comprehension (and the rabid right wing has happily jumped in to feed the greatest fears of its base: woke commie professors are poisoning the minds of the young!). A fundamental part of decolonizing knowledge today involves intellectual workers engaging in conscious, dramatic efforts to make ourselves seen and heard more effectively, in order to bring our work into the public sphere. This means developing and publicly practicing what Edward Said called "democratic criticism" in an all-too undemocratic time and place.

By the time we get to the end of this book, I hope to have you cheering for the end of the world—that is, specifically, the end of *this* world, so we can create that a new one.

Chapter Two

THE ENDS OF THE CULTURE WARS AND THE RISE OF INSTITUTIONAL MULTICULTURALISM, OR LEAVING EUROPE

Almost everyone agrees that multiculturalism is important, but almost nobody actually likes it. That sounds harsh, but think about it. For folks like me on what gets called "the left," "multiculturalism" is seen as an apolitical catchword used by administrators and corporate types who have no real interest in social justice. Since the 1990s, this institutional multiculturalism has become dominant, not just in universities but throughout much of the corporate world. Meanwhile, not unrelatedly, universities and the corporate world have been getting closer and closer together. This institutional multiculturalism is capitalist–friendly, controlled by administrators rather than students or teachers, and has little or nothing in common with true decolonization. It's not for nothing that radical critics such as Avery Gordon long ago identified institutional multiculturalism as a form of "diversity management"; its main goal is to limit, control, and ultimately cash in on depoliticized forms of diversity and difference.[1]

1   Avery Gordon, "The Work of Corporate Culture: Diversity Management," *Social Text* 44 (1995).

In the alternative universe inhabited by those on the right, however, it's a much different story. There, "multiculturalism" keeps company with the other scary words blared by Fox News to keep its elderly white viewers from dozing off: political correctness, wokeness, Communist indoctrination, BLM! For Fox rock star Tucker Carlson, the fact that the Buffalo school board now has an Office of Culturally & Linguistically Responsive Initiatives can mean only one thing: "By the time they hit high school, students in Buffalo are ready to go out into the world to destroy buildings and statues." Multiculturalism is a convenient villain for the right, since it can be trotted out and blamed for everything from looting in the streets to the War on Christmas to international terrorism to the plight of the so-called "white working class" to the supposed decline of the United States as a global force. It's the thing that needs to go if America is to be great again. If you were to say "multiculturalism" to the fascist paramilitary types who stormed Washington, D.C. in January 2021, they would surely bring out the nooses.

And that's exactly the problem: the relentless, decades-long right-wing onslaught against multiculturalism, even in its most milquetoast forms, has kept many of us would-be decolonizers in the position of defending it, even when we're reluctant to do so. Those attacks have become bolder, more terrifying, and more violent. The dominance of institutional multiculturalism, even in its current corporate-friendly, depoliticized form, has fed into the absurd but increasingly influential white suprem-acist claim that there is a need to defend "European culture" on campuses and in the larger public sphere. Openly racist groups like Identity Evropa re-brand their white supremacism as just another form of "identitarian-ism." For such groups, "European identity" needs to be defended against an all-powerful multiculturalism (as one of their slogans puts it: "Keep Your Diversity, We Want Identity").[2]

Multiculturalism is also a useful bogeyman for all sorts of right-wing politicians, from Donald Trump on down to the bottom-feeders who swim in his wake. Trump's administration carried on attacking multicul-turalism to the bitter end: on their last official day in office, Trump toady Mike Pompeo denounced multi-culturalism as "not who America is" and claimed that multiculturalist educators "distort our glorious found-ing." A day earlier, the Trump Administration had defaced Martin Luther King Day by releasing a report by its hand-picked "1776 Commission" that justified

2   See Alyssa Fisher, "What Is Identity Evropa?" *The Forward* (March 14, 2019).

slavery, defended the three-fifths compromise, and called for "patriotic education" to replace multicultural curricula in schools. The name of the commission is a thinly veiled reference to *The New York Times*' "1619 Project," which, together with a distorted caricature of "Critical Race Theory," has become an endless trough for racist trolls to feed upon.

And so it continues: take (please) the twenty-eight Republican legislators in Idaho who wrote an angry letter to the president of Boise State University complaining that the "drive to create a diversified and inclusive culture" and "support for multicultural student events" are "antithetical to the Idaho way." "We don't want funds expended for courses, programs, services, or trainings that confer support for extremist ideologies, such as those tied to social justice, racism, Marxism, socialism, or communism," fumed state representative Priscilla Giddings. In the face of threats to cut BSU's budget if the school didn't toe the line, administrators wilted in March 2021, suspending the university's lone mandatory diversity course, "Foundations of Ethics and Diversity," mid-semester.[3]

3   Nell Gluckman, "Why Did a University Suspend Its Mandatory Diversity Course?" *Chronicle of Higher Education* (March 18, 2021).

As I write this, at least five states have adopted statutes that outlaw the teaching of "critical race theory" and at least twenty-eight other states are currently considering similar laws. Such efforts (which don't even pretend to engage with the actual work of critical race theory) aim to stamp out any teaching that addresses (or even mentions) racial equity or white privilege; in essence, they criminalize anti-racist pedagogy. Meanwhile, Nikole Hannah-Jones, a Pulitzer Prize-winning journalist and one of the creators of the 1619 Project, had the offer of a tenured professorship at the University of North Carolina withdrawn by the Board of Trustees, thanks to attacks from right-wing commentators, donors, and politicos.[4]

For any of us concerned with decolonization, it's impossible not to feel compelled to take up the fight against these attacks on multiculturalism. But when we're spending all our time combatting absurd caricatures of "Critical Race Theory" by trolls who have never even heard of (never mind read) Kimberlé Crenshaw or Derrick Bell or Patricia Williams, or resisting the

4   See Cathryn Stout and Gabrielle LaMarr LeMee, "Efforts to Restrict Teaching About Racism and Bias Have Multiplied Across the U.S.," *Chalkbeat* (22 July 2021); Adam Serwer, "Why Conservatives Want to Cancel the 1619 Project," *The Atlantic* (May 21, 2021).

cancellation of required multicultural courses that we know to be woefully insufficient in the first place, or defending *The New York Times* (!), what has become of decolonization?

Leaving Europe

Let's pause and take stock of the situation. We might start by noting that "Europe" is a big word for the white supremacist types who won't abide multiculturalism even in its most insipid forms. That shouldn't be a surprise: decolonization has always aimed at this thing called Europe. It was from Europe that the modern crimes of conquest, dispossession, and genocide emanated, and it was in the name of Europe that these crimes were carried out. More than that: colonization *made* Europe. When Frantz Fanon declared that "Europe is literally the creation of the Third World," he meant that in the most material sense: both the raw materials (gold, diamonds, silver, oil, tea, coffee, spices, silk, cotton, timber) and the enslaved or indentured labor that shaped them was looted by Europeans from the rest of the world. But he also meant it in the larger philosophical sense: thanks to its economic, military, and political dominance over the world, Europe was able to make itself synonymous with "culture," and its colonies synonymous with barbarism."

(Stealing the world's cultural treasures and imprisoning them in European, and subsequently North American, museums and universities helped too.) That's why Fanon is clear about where decolonization needs to go, and why: "Let us leave this Europe which never stops talking of man yet massacres him at every one of its street corners, at every corner of the world."[5]

Multiculturalism, in its current institutional form, has most certainly *not* left this Europe. In fact, as much as we might hate the Eurocentrism of Identity Evropa and the 1776 Commission and those Idaho Republicans and Mike Fucking Pompeo, we should probably admit that when we're doing multiculturalism as it currently exists, Europe is still right in the middle of our thinking, where it's always been. The most common model of contemporary multiculturalism is the one that goes by the acronym DEI: Diversity, Equity, and Inclusion. Those are all good things. But the DEI approach is nevertheless indicative of everything that's wrong with institutional multiculturalism as it exists today, since every one of those words basically represents an *add-on* to Europe:

> *Diversity*: traditional European culture plus all those other places.

5   Frantz Fanon, *The Wretched of the Earth*, trans. Richard Philcox (New York: Grove, 2004), p. 58-59, 235.

Equity: all the good things that Europeans and Euro-Americans have always enjoyed, but now shared with others.

Inclusion: please let us in so we can share the goodies.

Even "multiculturalism" itself has a sort of winking relationship to the idea of Europe as the only true "culture": sure, there are lots of different cultures, and they are all worth celebrating, but European/Euro-American culture remains at the center. It is, after all, The Tradition, which multiculturalism aims only to diversify, equalize, and supplement via judicious inclusion of "the rest" alongside "the West."

If we want to get out of the vicious cycle of defending a multiculturalism that isn't working (and that we don't really want anyway) and start decolonizing multiculturalism instead, we need to begin by breaking down this "Europe" that we want to escape but can't seem to get away from. Cedric Robinson, the pioneering scholar of racial capitalism, can serve as an important guide here. In fact, to really understand what Robinson meant when he coined the term *racial capitalism* in his 1983 book *Black Marxism*, we need to begin by throwing away our usual understanding of the historical relationship between the West and "the rest." Generally, when people talk about racial capitalism (and they do so a lot these days—if you don't believe me, check out the hashtag #racialcapitalism on Instagram), they're trying to find a way to talk about how race and class are interconnected. The assumption is that "race" became a thing when Europeans went out into the world and encountered their "others" in the non-West. In this version of the story, whether they sailed east or west (or, for that matter, north or south), Europeans encountered those who looked, sounded, or acted differently than they did, and immediately went about racializing (and thereby inferiorizing) them. In a nutshell, that's the most common version of the story of how racism got invented. And that's why today, when many people say "racial capitalism," they mean: "capitalism, but I also want to talk about race so I'll add 'racial' to it."

But Robinson was getting at something deeper and more earth-shattering. The story he tells in the dense and difficult but mind-blowing pages of *Black Marxism* reveals that the process of what we would now call "racializing" originally happened *between Europeans*, largely as a result of intra-European slavery and indentured servitude. The age of European colonialism, beginning in the fifteenth century, is often seen as the moment when racism was "invented." But Robinson begins his story almost two thousand years before that—with Aristotle, that great pillar of "our"

Western tradition (although Aristotle was born in the Greek city of Stagira and lived out much of his life on the island of Euboea, both of which are a heck of a lot closer to Africa than they are to, say, London or New York or Toronto). Aristotle's concept of "Natural Law," a defining concept for European thought, declares slaves, women, laborers of every kind, and in fact all non-Greeks to be inherently inferior. In other words, thousands of years before the European age of colonialism, Aristotle had already "articulated an uncompromising racial construct."[6]

When defenders of "our" European tradition number Aristotle among the founding fathers—along with Plato, Socrates, Pythagoras, and the rest of the "Greeks"—they are of course being wildly ahistorical. While the word "Europe" can be traced back to ancient Greece, it wasn't really used to describe the geographical territory that we now think of as "Europe" until the eighth or ninth century CE, and the term "European" wasn't used until the beginning of the seventeenth century. The reason for backdating the "European tradition" to the Greeks, of course, is to give it a sense of

6   Cedric J. Robinson, *Black Marxism: The Making of the Black Radical Tradition* (Chapel Hill: University of North Carolina Press, 2000), p. xxxi.

timeless authority—the same way scam artists break and scuff up broken pieces of pottery to fool naïve buyers into thinking they're "ancient artifacts."

Though he would never have considered himself to be "European," Aristotle became hugely important to the development of European culture once his writings began to be translated into Latin in the twelfth century. However, this "recovery" of Aristotle by European scholars was only made possible by an earlier set of Muslim scholars who had preserved his work via Arabic translation. As the philosopher Peter Adamson has noted, "In tenth-century Baghdad, readers of Arabic had about the same degree of access to Aristotle that readers of English do today."[7] This is something the white supremacist defenders of "European culture" do *not* want to talk about.

As Robinson unfolds his story of the development of racial capitalism, we see how Aristotle's "racial calculus" determines the very nature of what "Europe" comes to be: "from the twelfth century on, one European ruling order after another, one cohort of clerical or secular

7   See Peter Adamson, *Philosophy in the Islamic World* (New York: Oxford University Press, 2016) and "Arabic Translators Did Far More Than Just Preserve Greek Philosophy," *Aeon* (November 4, 2016).

propagandists following another, reiterated and embellished this racial calculus."[8] That means racialist thinking—or let's be clearer and call it what it is: rac*ism*—is not only older than European colonialism; it is older than capitalism, and indeed older than Europe itself.

Racism, in short, doesn't begin when Europe goes out into the world and meets its Other. It starts in Europe among Europeans, and "has its genesis in the 'internal' relations of European peoples."[9] That long history means that capitalism has *always* been racial. Europe doesn't encounter its racial other out there in the "non-West" (wherever that is); it finds it within itself, among those whom it has enslaved or otherwise subjugated, and then keeps finding its Others wherever it goes in the world—at every one of its street corners, at every corner of the world, like Fanon says.

Painted Statues and Racist Trolls

So now we can return to today's battles around multiculturalism armed with a different set of weapons. Drawing on the work he carried out in *Black Marxism*, Robinson wrote a series of essays in the 1980s arguing that, far

8   Robinson, *Black Marxism*, p. xxxi.

9   Robinson, *Black Marxism*, p. 2.

from being a trendy new thing, "multiculturalism" has actually existed for thousands of years—but only in a *negative* form, more specifically "as a construction of contamination" (think: barbarians at the gates).[10] That's how this thing called Europe—and, more generally, "the West"—invented itself, by pointing towards those other, inferior cultures and identifying itself as their opposite. If you think about it, "Identity Evropa" itself is a meaningless term without an inferior other against which to define itself. So even the white supremacists, at the end of the day, need multiculturalism, if only to define those "other" cultures that they claim to be different from and better than. All those defenders of "our Western tradition" have no problem agreeing that Western culture isn't the *only* culture; but they insist that it's the *best* culture, and thus the only one that really matters. They're multiculturalists too—just really bad ones.

Needless to say, according to this simple-minded logic, "European" is interchangeable with "white." The urgency that defenders of the "Western tradition" feel about keeping this equation (European = white) from being questioned is evident in the violent response that

10   Cedric J. Robinson, "Ota Benga's Flight Through Geronimo's Eyes: Tales of Science and Multiculturalism," in Goldberg, *Multiculturalism*, p. 389.

the fascist right has had even to scholarly debates over the issue. For example, a professor of classics, Sarah Bond, has written several articles refuting the idea that Greco-Roman sculptures were unpainted white marble. In fact, as she notes, modern technology has revealed that these statues were usually painted, using colors such as gold, red, green, black, white, and brown, but they have, over time, faded to their base marble color. So when museums and textbooks present an array of ancient sculptures in a state of "neon whiteness," among other things, it "serves to create a false idea of homogeneity—everyone was very white!—across the Mediterranean region."[11]

Although classical scholars have presented both historical and scientific evidence, the equation of stark white marble with aesthetic perfection has persisted. Bond describes visiting a museum with a friend who, upon seeing painted marble statues, exclaimed: "There is no way the Greeks were that gauche." This reflexive response is so hard to break because for centuries, the supposed "whiteness" of these classical statues became

11   Sarah E. Bond, "Whitewashing Ancient Statues: Whiteness, Racism and Color in the Ancient World," *Forbes* (April 27, 2017) and "Why We Need to Start Seeing the Classical World in Color," *Hyperallergic* (June 7, 2017).

a way to shape and uphold a white standard of beauty. In fact, as any art historian can tell you, many white marble statues from ancient Rome are in fact copies of Greek originals that were sculpted in bronze. The preference of Roman artists for marble rather than bronze would be familiar to artists anywhere: by the height of the Roman Empire, marble was simply cheaper and easier to find. But seventeenth- and eighteenth-century art historians—most prominently the German Johann Joachim Winckelmann, sometimes called the father of art history—canonized the idea that these white statues were the epitome of human beauty. Europeans could trace their descent to these perfect white marble ancestors; by contrast, Winckelmann was fond of denigrating the appearance of various non-Europeans as "irregular" and thus "an offense against beauty." As in life, so it was in art: "color in sculpture came to mean barbarism, for they assumed that the lofty ancient Greeks were too sophisticated to color their art."[12]

Whiteness was beautiful, and Europeans were, of course, white; all was right with the world.

These notions of white beauty are still a powerful influence on white supremacy today. While scholars

12 Nell Irvin Painter, *The History of White People* (New York: W.W. Norton, 2010), p. 60-62.

have come to accept the reality of painted statues as a fact, defenders of white Europe still need the false but stark sense of homogeneity that you can get by looking at ancient white sculptures. Yes, they insist, everyone was very white! That's why, for her scholarly pains, Bond found herself an object of abuse by right-wing attack sites like *National Review* and *Campus Reform*, which in turn led to online attacks from right-wing trolls, including demands for her termination, antisemitic slurs, and threats of violence.[13] While she may thus hold the distinction of being one of very few scholars of the classical world to receive death threats based on her scholarship, she is hardly alone. Other scholars who have pushed back against the deployment of homogenized versions of medieval European history by white supremacists have received similar threats. Dorothy Kim, a distinguished scholar of medieval literature, wrote a piece called "Teaching Medieval Studies in a Time of White Supremacy" in the days following the white supremacist riot in Charlottesville in 2017, calling on her colleagues to resist the "weaponization" of medieval Europe by the far right. In response, she too was subjected to a

---

13   See Colleen Flaherty, "Threats for What She Didn't Say," *Inside Higher Education* (June 19, 2017).

right-wing campaign of harassment, including death threats.[14]

When scholars addressing such rarified topics as Roman statues and medieval literature become the targets of Trump-loving trolls, it means they've hit a nerve. But while scholar after scholar has ably debunked the myth of a monolithic, "white" European culture, it continues to define debates about multiculturalism. That's in part because it gets echoed and harnessed by such powerful political figures as Steve King, who served as a US congressman for seventeen years before finally being defeated in 2020. "The idea of multiculturalism, that every culture is equal—that's not objectively true," King frothed, back in 2016. "We've been fed that information for the past twenty-five years, and we're not going to become a greater nation if we continue to do that."[15] That's a pretty good distillation of the ideology that drives Trumpism.

14   Dorothy Kim, "Teaching Medieval Studies in a Time of White Supremacy," *In the Middle* (August 28, 2017); Chauncey DeVega, "Alt-Right Catches Knight Fever—But Medieval Scholars Strike Back," *Salon* (November 30, 2017).

15   Amber Phillips, "Steve King: The Idea that Every Culture Is Equal Is 'Not Objectively True,'" *Washington Post* (July 20, 2016).

Crawling from the Ruins of the Culture Wars

If you do the math, that twenty-five years that Congress-man King referred to (perhaps counting on his fingers and toes to reach such a high number) takes us back to the beginning of the 1990s. Without saying it out loud, he's clearly referring to the period marked by the so-called "culture wars" of the eighties and nineties. Depending on who you ask, you'll get different explanations of what those "wars" were about and what was at stake in them. In a nutshell, the phrase refers to a series of political battles fought over what generally get described as "cultural" issues. But even the question of what counts as "cultural" is up for grabs when it comes to the culture wars. In some cases, that cultural context was readily apparent. For example, there was a massive political debate (culminating in a Supreme Court decision) over whether federal funding for "controversial" (read: politically radical and/or queer) artists like Andres Serrano, Karen Finley, and Robert Mapplethorpe was important for supporting the free expression of artists or, rather, was a waste of taxpayer money on work that was "immoral" and therefore un-American. In other instances, the description of certain struggles—for example, those carried on by the feminist and queer liberation movements, opposed tooth and nail by conservatives—as "cultural" has sometimes been a condescending way of separating them from so-called "real" politics.[16]

For readers too young to have lived through the culture wars (and for those of us old enough to remember but who have preferred to forget the details), Andrew Hartman's 2005 book *A War for the Soul of America: A History of the Culture Wars* provides a useful summary of the standard story:

> The culture wars were battles over what constituted art, and over whether the federal government should subsidize art that insulted the most cherished beliefs of millions of Americans. The culture wars were debates over transgressive films and television shows, and over whether insensitive cultural programming should be censored. They were brawls over the public schools, and over whether American children should learn divisive subjects like evolutionary biology. They involved struggles over the university curriculum, and over whether American college students should read a traditional Western canon or texts that represented a more diverse range of perspectives. The culture wars were fights over how the nation's history was narrated in museums, and over whether the purpose of American history was to make Americans

16 See Lisa Duggan and Nan D. Hunter, *Sex Wars: Sexual Dissent and Political Culture* (New York: Routledge, 1995).

proud of the nation's glorious past or to encourage citizens to reflect on its moral failings.[17]

Hartman's book takes its title from a phrase uttered by Patrick Buchanan during a raucous speech at the 1992 Republican National Convention. Buchanan was part of a rogues' gallery of right-wing demagogues who made their careers as cultural warriors during the eighties and nineties, from "Moral Majority" founder Jerry Falwell to Ivy League poster boy and future felon Dinesh D'Souza to "Bachelor Jeff" Christie, a young drive-time radio DJ who decided to go back to using his given name for his latest career move as a right-wing talk show host: Rush Limbaugh. No wonder Buchanan, who rode the waves of the culture wars so effectively that he almost unseated George H. W. Bush as the Republican presidential candidate in 1992, declared that "culture is the Ho Chi Minh Trail to power."[18]

According to this standard account of the culture wars, most of its battles were eventually won by those on the left—that is, by and large, by multiculturalists.

17   Andrew Hartman, *A War for the Soul of America: A History of the Culture Wars* (Chicago: University of Chicago Press, 2015), p. 15.

18   John Dillin, "Conservative Republicans Call for 'Culture War,'" *Christian Science Monitor* (May 17, 1993), quoted in Hartman, *A War for the Soul of America*, p. 16.

While the right had its share of victories in the realms of economic policy and electoral politics, in the sphere of culture—the terrain upon which the culture wars were fought—the left ultimately prevailed. By this account, while the war dragged on for a couple of decades, in the end, "multiculturalism" won a decisive victory. Even some conservatives agreed: in 1998, the neoconservative intellectual Nathan Glazer, no friend of multicultural-ism, published *We Are All Multiculturalists Now*, ruefully admitting that multiculturalism was here to stay (though not everyone on the right was ready to surrender— Dinesh D'Souza accused Glazer of "cowardice" and of having spent too much time hanging around Harvard). The election of Barack Obama in 2008 was seen as the culmination of this victory, marking the commence-ment of American's new fully multicultural era. Liberal pundits (and even Obama himself, early in his presi-dency) started to speak seriously about the United States entering a "post-racial" era. According to the script, Obama's two terms in office were to be followed seam-lessly by the election of his Secretary of State, Hillary Clinton, at which point we would be able to check sex-ism off the list too.

In the event, of course, Donald J. Trump drove his evil clown car straight through that triumphal nar-rative. Trump's skillful manipulation of the story of multiculturalism's victory is part of the reason why he won. But the fact that liberal commentators were almost universally blindsided by Trump's ascendance also suggests that there was always something very wrong with that story itself.

The Culture Wars and the War on the Poor

You'll get a very different version of the culture wars and their lasting effects if you view them from a different perspective: that of working-class communities of color. The culture wars, far from ushering in the perpetual peace of universal multiculturalism, were experienced by these communities as part of a direct attack on them. If the eighties and nineties were a period when arts funding and "political correctness" and curricular changes were being debated, it was also a time when the victories won by the Civil Rights movement came under attack, when Black electoral gains began to be reversed, and when both economic inequality and state violence against communities of color increased dramatically—a trend that has worsened catastrophically in the first two decades of the twenty-first century. For communities devastated by these attacks, it didn't take the election of Donald Trump to put the lie to the idea that America had become a "post-racial" society; the day to day reality of the previous forty years had made this starkly clear.

But surely the culture wars were one thing, and the political and economic wars being carried out against working class communities of color were part of a very different process—you know, *real* politics? That's only true if you limit the scope of what the culture wars were (and are) to questions like "whether or not Cleopatra was black, or if multicultural education constitutes a new form of academic tyranny," to quote Robin Kelley's brilliant book *Yo' Mama's Disfunktional! Fighting the Culture Wars in Urban America*.[19] In fact, as Kelley argues, there were other cultural battlefields: for example, the "ghetto ethnographies" by social scientists that flattened the complexity of Black expressive cultures and communities into the convenient category of "the underclass." This was an extension of the narrative set in motion by Daniel Patrick Moynihan's 1965 report *The Negro Family: The Case for National Action*, which put much of the blame for poverty in working class communities of color on the supposed "dysfunction" of Black families, particularly single-parent families.

This cultural narrative was then put to work by neoconservatives to undo affirmative action programs intended to fight racism and to attack forms of public

19 Robin D. G. Kelley, *Yo' Mama's Disfunktional! Fighting the Culture Wars in Urban America* (Boston: Beacon Press, 1997), p. 3.

assistance set up to fight poverty. As a result, at the same moment when battles to establish multicultural curricula were being won, the larger public discourse was dominated by racist cultural stereotypes: the centuries-old stereotype of "the lazy, irresponsible Negro," but articulated in a new cultural vocabulary: "the underclass," "matriarchy," "welfare queens," "criminals," "dysfunctional."[20]

Both the ghetto ethnographers who helped invent "the underclass" and Daniel Patrick Moynihan himself—a member of President Lyndon Johnson's "War on Poverty" team and later a long-serving democratic senator from New York—were liberals, not right-wingers. Grasping that fact is the key to understanding how the culture wars and the war on Black working-class communities came together to help create our current form of multiculturalism. After all, it was a Democrat—one William Jefferson Clinton—who presided over "the end of welfare as we know it," denying key forms of public assistance to millions of poor families. Clinton's presidency also coincides neatly with the final years of the culture wars (1992-2000) and the declared victory of the multiculturalist left.

20   Kelley, *Yo' Mama's Disfunktional!*, p. 8.

If you want to understand the cultural aspect of Clinton's war on the poor, just play the name game with me. The most significant program targeted by Clinton's "welfare reform" initiative was called the Aid to Families with Dependent Children (AFDC) program, established by the Social Security Act of 1935. The replacement program set up by Clinton's plan—which imposed a five-year lifetime limit on welfare assistance, as well as a draconian permanent lifetime ban on eligibility for anyone convicted of a felony drug offense—was given a name that replaced the neutrality of AFDC with a harsh and scolding tone that fit the nature of the "reforms" being imposed: it was now to be known as the "Temporary Assistance to Needy Families" program. And the name of Clinton's signature bill that made all this possible? "The Personal Responsibility and Work Opportunity Reconciliation Act." These were political and economic initiatives, but it's impossible to imagine them gaining momentum without the help of cultural keywords produced by the culture wars of the eighties and nineties: "welfare queens," "the underclass," "personal responsibility," "dysfunctional families," "criminals."

Another legacy of the culture war on the poor coalesced during Clinton's presidency: the massive expansion of the Prison Industrial Complex. Here too there is an important cultural aspect. The end of the culture wars and the perceived victory of multiculturalism was supposed to bring the United States into a new "post-racial" era. But as Michelle Alexander argues in *The New Jim Crow: Mass Incarceration in the Age of Colorblindness*, the only thing that changed were the names. In the new age of "colorblindness" that followed the culture wars, "it is no longer socially permissible to use race, explicitly, as a justification for discrimination, exclusion, and social contempt." Instead, the structural racism inherent in the criminal justice system performs a cultural sleight of hand: labeling people of color "criminals" and then carrying on with precisely the same forms of racial discrimination that flourished under Jim Crow. After all, once the label "felon" is affixed, all the traditional Jim Crow practices, including "employment discrimination, housing discrimination, denial of the right to vote, denial of educational opportunity, denial of food stamps and other public benefits, and exclusion from jury service," are all perfectly legal. Words like "criminal" and "felon" are also, of course, "colorblind" terminology, and therefore outside the jurisdiction of multiculturalism.[21]

---

21   Michelle Alexander, *The New Jim Crow: Mass Incarceration in the Age of Colorblindness* (New York: New Press, 2010), p. 2.

As the Clinton Administration, and with it the twentieth century, came to an end, the whole system of social safety nets for poor communities lay in ruins and the ideology of "law and order," once the watchwords of rabid segregationists and right-wing vigilantes, was firmly entrenched in the liberal mainstream. At the same time, Clinton's White House could celebrate his embrace of multiculturalism by trumpeting the fact that the President had "appointed the most diverse Cabinet in history": seven African Americans served as Cabinet Secretaries and nearly half his Cabinet were women, including the first women to serve as Secretary of State (Madeline Albright) and Attorney General (Janet Reno), along with the first Asian American to serve in a Cabinet (Commerce Secretary Norman Mineta). Clinton's appointment of African Americans, Latinos, and women to federal judgeships were also lauded, along with his commitment to having "people with disabilities" serve throughout his administration.

It is only by understanding the overlap between these two realities—Clinton engineered and oversaw an explicitly racist war against the poor *and* simultaneously carried out exemplary policies of multicultural diversity within his administration—that we can begin to dig ourselves out from under the rubble of the culture wars to understand where we find ourselves today.

Multicultural Capitalist Realism

Here, then, is a different summary of the culture wars and their aftermath: the counter-cultural energy released by political movements in the 1960s slammed up against the 1980s, the era of Ronald Reagan and Margaret Thatcher. In the ensuing battles, the left won its share of cultural victories, often in the name of "multicultural-ism," at the same moment that the economic policies of neoliberalism were effectively locked into place, when socialism was declared dead, and when history—so we were told—came to an end. Institutional multicultural-ism was what remained standing at the culmination of a long and violent counterinsurgency campaign by the US state and corporations against the material and political gains won by the social movements of the 1960s and 1970s. Clinton's war on the poor brought together the austerity policies of neoliberalism and the cultural poli-tics of "colorblind" racism, even as he was able to point to his exemplarily "diverse" cabinet to prove that he was following the rules of the new institutional multicultur-alism that emerged triumphant from the culture wars.

And that's where we find ourselves today: in educa-tional institutions, in electoral politics, in the media, and in the corporate world, multiculturalism is now a cru-cial part of what Mark Fisher called "capitalist realism."

Capitalist realism, which Fischer describes as being not so much an argument or an ideology as it is "a pervasive atmosphere" that functions "as a kind of invisible barrier constraining thought and action," insists that the world created by the neoliberal policies of Reagan and Thatcher and their allies is not only the best of all possible worlds but in fact the only realistic possibility.[22] Britain's Iron Lady summed it up with brutal clarity in one of her favorite phrases: "there is no alternative." Thatcher didn't just mean that capitalism was the only system that worked; she meant it was now the only system, full stop. The "liberal" alternatives to Reagan and Thatcher, Bill Clinton and Tony Blair, were equally in thrall to capitalist realism but were able to add a soupçon of multiculturalism—austerity with a touch of diversity! In its current institutional forms, multiculturalism continues to comply with the rules of capitalist realism.

There is of course an alternative to capitalist realism. One of its names is decolonization. But that also means that our current neoliberal version of multiculturalism—the sort that allows you to attack working class communities of color while draping yourself in your commitment to "diversity"—isn't the only alternative.

22 Mark Fisher, *Capitalist Realism: Is There No Alternative?* (London: Zer0 Books, 2009), p. 16.

Another alternative can be found in the vision Robin Kelley set against Clintonism back in the late 1990s: "The hope and future of America lie with the very multicolored working class that for so long has been seen as the problem rather than the solution."[23] Consider the book you are reading to be marching under that flag as well.

23   Kelley, *Yo' Mama's Disfunktional!*, p. 12-13.

Chapter Three

MULTICULTURALISM VERSUS MONOCULTURALISM, OR BUILD THAT WALL! [WITH GREAT BOOKS]

You may have noticed that I haven't yet offered any definitive definition of "multiculturalism." I'm sorry to disappoint, but by and large, I'm not going to. For the project of decolonization, it's more important to try to understand what multiculturalism *does* than what it claims to be. In any case, "multiculturalism" has always been a moving target; since the term first started to come into wide use in the 1980s, its meanings have changed and shifted. And as we saw in the last chapter, today the question of what multiculturalism is depends on where you're standing, and who you're standing with.

In fact, the best scholars of multiculturalism begin by noting that no one can really agree about what it is in the first place—and the more the term gets used, the more confusing things get. Avery Gordon and Christopher Newfield begin their essential 1996 collection *Mapping Multiculturalism* by noting that as the term "has appeared more and more frequently in current social and cultural debates, its meanings have become less and less clear." A dozen years later, Shirley R. Steinberg says essentially the same thing in her preface to *Diversity and Multiculturalism: A Reader*: "Over the past couple of decades, Western societies have debated the question of multiculturalism with surprisingly little agreement over the meaning of the term." Even Ali Rattansi's excellent *Multiculturalism: A Very Short Introduction* notes how hard it is to actually "introduce" multiculturalism, since "an acceptable definition of multiculturalism has been notoriously elusive." "Perhaps what is clearest in recent public debates about multiculturalism," he concludes, "is that not much is clear when it comes to the key terms involved."[1]

More helpfully, Rattansi notes the important difference between using the term "multicultural" descriptively—for example, to denote multiethnic societies—as against the "-ism" version, which he describes as "the policy response to the diversity created in increasingly multicultural (multiethnic) societies." In other words, while "multicultural" can be used in a straightforwardly descriptive way, "multicultural*ism*" is by its nature a *political* word. David Theo Goldberg makes a similar point, differentiating between "multicultural

1   Avery F. Gordon and Christopher Newfield, eds. *Mapping Multiculturalism* (Minneapolis: University of Minnesota Press, 1996), p. 1; Shirley R. Steinberg, ed. *Diversity and Multiculturalism: A Reader* (New York: Peter Lang, 2009), p. xi; Ali Rattansi, *Multiculturalism: A Very Short Introduction* (New York: Oxford University Press, 2011), p. 7.

conditions"—the various forms of lived expression and experience that mark our historical moment—versus "multicultural*ism*," an ideological term that has generally been used to reduce, fix, and ultimately simplify that larger set of lived conditions into a single definable thing.[2] Neoliberal institutions have a very real and very material interest in this sort of reducing, fixing, and simplifying of complex multicultural conditions, which may be why institutional multiculturalism has been such a useful tool for diversity management.

But if "multiculturalism" is by its nature a political word, that also means that it's up for grabs. The politics of multiculturalism is not necessarily embedded in the word itself. If it's true that the most prominent forms of institutional multiculturalism today perform a capitalist-friendly and ultimately counterrevolutionary sort of work, that doesn't mean that the word can't carry a very different sort of political charge. In other words, we need to differently politicize multiculturalism in order to take it back and add it to our radical toolbox.

2   Rattansi, *Multiculturalism*, p. 12; David Theo Goldberg,
     ed. *Multiculturalism: A Critical Reader* (Cambridge:
     Blackwell, 1994), p. 1.

Follow the Invisible Line: The Rise of
Monoculturalism and the Birth of MAGA

Multiculturalism has an opposite number against which it has had to fight: *monoculturalism*. If that's not a term we tend to use today, it's not because it isn't still present or powerful. Quite the contrary: we don't talk about "monoculturalism" precisely because its project has been so successful—that is, because it has been sold to us as, simply, capital-C Culture: "the best that has been thought and said."

In the US context, we can trace the development of a specifically "American" monoculturalism back to the nineteenth century. The settler colonists who had recently won their political independence from the British and were still in the process of carrying forward the wholesale theft of a continent from its native peoples needed a culture to fit their "new" country. American culture, as we continue to know it today, came out of this need to "create the impression of an intellectual tradition where there was indeed none."[3] This need to create an "American" intellectual tradition out of thin air in turn came from the fact that the actual indigenous

3   David Theo Goldberg, ed. *Multiculturalism: A Critical Reader* (Cambridge: Blackwell, 1994), p. 3.

cultural and intellectual traditions of the Americas—the traditions of the peoples who were living in these lands before they were "discovered" by Europeans—were violently suppressed (though never totally destroyed) by European settler colonialism.[4] The final product of this attempt to create a monocultural ("American") intellectual tradition is the misshapen creature that conservatives like to call, simply, "Western civilization."

Think about it this way: a white male literature professor (like me) can, if he wants, stand in front of a classroom anywhere in the US today and talk about "our Western tradition," "Western civilization," or, simply, "The Great Books." He just needs to draw an invisible line. He'll begin by going all the way back to ancient Greece (if he's starting with Homer's *Iliad*—and he probably is—he's actually beginning in Troy, in what we now call Turkey, but he'll feel no need to mention that), thence through Rome (again, don't call attention to all the North African and Middle Eastern locales in the works of Virgil and Ovid), skipping over those inconvenient centuries during which the Arab World and Africa were the intellectual centers (he'll just refer to

4   See M. Annette Jaimes Guerrero, "Academic Apartheid: American Indian Studies and 'Multiculturalism,'" in Gordon and Newfield, *Mapping Multiculturalism*, p. 49-63.

those as the "Dark Ages") straight to "The Renaissance" (keeping the bloodiest details about the Crusades and the Catholic inquisitions on the down-low, and never mentioning the beginning of European imperialism, the genocide visited upon the Americas, or the beginnings of the Euro-American chattel slave trade), catching a ride with Chaucer, Boccaccio, Cervantes, and the French troubadours, absorbing the resonant rhythms of the King James Bible (Jesus spoke English, didn't he?), going to the theater with Shakespeare, Molière, and Goethe, jumping on a ship with Melville (we might spot Henry James sailing in the opposite direction), who takes us to Twain, who ferries us to Faulkner, who's a neighbor of T. S. Eliot, who knows everybody on both sides of the Atlantic and introduces us to them all—The Tradition, which is from everywhere and nowhere all at once but which is nevertheless "ours" thanks to this insane, genocidal, completely irrational collective act of intellectual gerrymandering.

That hypothetical professor (and he's still thriving, trust me) would never call himself a "monoculturalist," and he would certainly blanch even whiter if you were to accuse him of being a white supremacist. Nor would he ever describe himself as teaching "monocultural literature." He just teaches The Great Books. Why? Perhaps because he agrees, on some level, with the argument provided by former secretary of education and forever cultural warrior William Bennett in *To Reclaim a Legacy*, the report that he authored for the National Endowment for the Humanities in 1983, in the opening days of the culture wars. "The Great Books," Bennett insists, represent "the glue that binds together our pluralistic nation." Bennett squares the circle with a leap of logic that seems inevitable but, if you think about it for a minute, actually manages to render the word "Western" totally meaningless: "The fact that we as Americans—whether black or white, Asian or Hispanic, rich or poor—share these beliefs aligns us with other cultures of the Western tradition."[5]

Allow me to draw a different invisible line than the one that traces the contours of this supposed "Western tradition." This line follows the echo of Bennett's resounding call to "reclaim a legacy" over the course of three or four decades, until we find ourselves in the presence of a crowd shouting out a more ferocious battle cry: "Make America Great Again!" This is where we currently find ourselves, and even though our hypothetical

5   William Bennett, *To Reclaim a Legacy: A Report on the Humanities in Higher Education* (Washington, DC: National Endowment for the Humanities [NEH], 1984), p. 38.

professor is a gentle and cultured soul who likely detests Donald Trump as a vulgarian and would curl his lip at anyone wearing a MAGA cap, we would never have gotten a Trump presidency without this gentleman's help.

The Muddy Shoes of Politics

There are a few important takeaways from this brief history of "monoculturalism." First: monoculturalism is a political invention—a fairly recent one in the United States, though a bit older elsewhere. Second: monoculturalism's best trick is to turn itself invisible, which is to say, to declare itself universal. "Transcendent" is a favorite word for this; if The Great Books, and art more generally, inhabits a plane above and beyond ordinary human existence, then mere social categories like race or gender or class are, we're told, irrelevant. This allows the monoculturalist to paint multiculturalists as parochial and priggish—*you* all keep talking about race and class and gender and imperialism and blah blah blah, *we* just want to talk about Great Books, which are transcendent and thus devoid of race, i.e. Western, i.e. white. Third: monoculturalism's trump card (so to speak) is to make this whole process appear to be totally divorced from politics. *We* just want to teach universally great culture, but *you* multiculturalists keep dragging your muddy shoes of politics through our nice clean seminar rooms.

As we saw in the previous chapter, for white supremacists—not just those who proudly identify as such but also those who, like our hypothetical litera- ture professor, would indignantly deny being any such thing—the "Western" in Western culture is synony- mous with "white." That has a history too, one told by historians like Nell Irvin Painter, David Roediger, and Noel Ignatiev as the invention of "whiteness." But alongside this emerging thing called whiteness arose a more frightening specter, what Cedric Robinson iden- tifies as the "myth of white solidarity" that played a key role in the founding of American monoculture: "It was for the most part a lie, but a terribly seductive one. By the end of the nineteenth century it had already substan- tially displaced the past and mystified the relations of the day. It remains in place."[6] The specter of white solidarity is of course palpable at a Trump rally, but it also hovers over every classroom where someone is teaching The Great Books as "our" American tradition.

This leads us to one more historical takeaway: if American monoculturalism had to be invented from scratch in the nineteenth century, that means that there's nothing necessarily *new* about multiculturalism. After all,

6   Cedric Robinson, *Black Marxism: The Making of the Black Radical Tradition* (Chapel Hill: U of North Carolina P, 2000), p. 80-81.

what is the "mono" in monoculturalism if not a wall meant to keep out "foreign" cultures? This realization opens new possibilities for thinking about what multiculturalism is, what it has done, and what it might begin to do differently. Radical critics have insisted that the "West" only exists by defining itself against what it is *not*. Indeed, you can say that Edward Said's world-changing book *Orientalism* is a patient unfolding of the story by which a round globe was divided into a "West" and an "East," which were then seen as obvious "facts" that would guide all subsequent common sense: after all, East is East and West is West, and so on and so on.

This is all to say that multiculturalism has *always* been a part of "the West," but for centuries, this was a *negative* multiculturalism. As we saw in the previous chapter, you can trace this negative version all the way back to Aristotle. "Premodern multiculturalism" was based on explicit notions of superiority and inferiority—the sorts of "natural" differences that Aristotle used to justify slavery and the subordination of women. "Modernist multiculturalism," which comes into being alongside the age of European imperialism, the global slave trade, and capitalism, simply extends this already-existing premodern story about multiculturalism as a matter of superior and inferior cultures, using philosophy, literature, historiography, and science to ground this supposed inferiority in the sort of "knowledge" that Said calls Orientalism. In doing so, it takes the process a step further, making European superiority universal by "posit[ing] the West as *the* civilization and the European white as *the* conscious agency of humanity's historical development."[7]

When it came time to create a new American monoculture on a Turtle Island bloodied by genocidal conquest, what better way to do this than by hitching the American star to this narrative of "Western" superiority and inferiority? From Aristotle on down: that's us! You won't hear a lot about Aristotle at a Trump rally, but it's still the same old story.

That's a lot of history that we're left to fight against. If multiculturalism is to be a weapon for this fight, we'll need to find a way to harness the centuries-old reality of multicultural conditions into a critical multiculturalism capable of fighting not just against the myth of monoculturalism, but against its foundation in the old story of superior and inferior cultures. That story continues to create the fear that the "great" culture of the West will be contaminated by contact with those bad "other" cultures of the rest. For our literature professor, that might

7   Cedric J. Robinson, "Ota Benga's Flight Through Geronimo's Eyes: Tales of Science and Multiculturalism," in Goldberg, *Multiculturalism*, p. 388-89.

mean building a Great Books program; for Trump's minions, it means building The Wall. One leads inexorably to the other.

Rolling Canons into the Classroom, or Who Won the Literary Canon Wars?

In fact, another way of telling the story of how our existing form of institutional multiculturalism gained ascendance is by seeing it as yet another chapter in the centuries-long story of monoculturalism. To put it more bluntly: institutional multiculturalism is simply the latest and most efficient model of white supremacy.

What today passes as "multiculturalism" became dominant in universities and other institutions largely as a result of the culture wars of the 1980s and 1990s. One much-discussed battlefield were the "literary canon wars": a struggle, fought largely by writers and critics and teachers but also by politicians and pundits who fancied themselves culture warriors, over which literary works should be read and taught in schools. The use of the word "canon" here is significant: in its original usage, it referred to laws or regulations issued by religious authorities, and subsequently to the creation of authoritative lists of texts that were considered "scripture." It was only in the nineteenth century—right around the time that "American" monoculture was being invented—that "canon" began to be used in a secular sense, to describe an authoritative list of works sanctioned as "great literature."

Which texts and writers deserved to be enshrined in the canon? For conservatives eager to defend a monocultural "American" tradition, it was simple: you could just draw an equal sign between "the canon of great literature" and "the Western tradition." The clearest articulation of this position was in a 1994 book by the dean of conservative literary critics, Harold Bloom: *The Western Canon.* The conventional story of the literary canon wars goes like this: defenders of the Western canon, like Bloom, fought to keep that canon intact; meanwhile, proponents of multiculturalism insisted on the inclusion of writers who didn't fit the profile of "dead white men"—that is, they were fighting to expand the canon in order to make it more inclusive. From this perspective, multiculturalism ultimately won the war, since the literary canon—or, at least, the reading lists for many high schools and colleges—has indeed been, in many cases, expanded.

Twenty years later, the deaths, within a few months of each other, of canon defender Harold Bloom and Nobel Prize-winning novelist Toni Morrison gave

The New York Times an opportunity to do a simplistic and sloppy postmortem of the canon wars. Looking back to the early days of the war, we're told, "Mr. Bloom and Ms. Morrison stood on opposite sides of a cultural debate about what to read in college and, more broadly, about how to read." So, who won? The *Times'* verdict on the outcome of this war is rendered in typical lukewarm-pundit style: Morrison and Bloom both sort of won, and they both sort of lost. On the one hand, the authors and texts upheld by Bloom as central to the Western tradition continue to dominate most high school and college reading lists, so the canon has remained mostly intact. But at the same time, the canon had indeed expanded and had become more inclusive, so multiculturalists could also claim victory. Somehow, it took two people to write this silly article.[8]

What's more important than this inconclusive conclusion is how these two pundits—Joe Karaganis and David McClure—arrived at it. Neither of them is a critic, writer, or teacher of literature: Karaganis is a sociologist and McClure a computer scientist; both work

8   Joe Karaganis and David McClure, "Did Harold Bloom or Toni Morrison Win the Literary Canon Wars?" *The New York Times* (October 19, 2019). The article's subtitle sort of says it all: "It wasn't Bloom. But it wasn't not Bloom, either."

at the Open Syllabus Project, which describes itself as "the first 'big data' look at the primary activity of higher education: teaching." Basically, they collect course syllabi—millions of them, apparently—and then crunch the numbers. I can't say that the results are particularly scintillating: for example, the list of books most often assigned by professors is topped by (drumroll!) style manuals for beginning writers—William Strunk's *Elements of Style* takes the crown—which isn't exactly a revelation. However, Karaganis and McClure seem quite certain that data alone will prevent any future canon-war skirmishes. After all, back in the Neanderthal days of the 1980s, "no one knew what was actually being assigned and taught," whereas happily, today we've got the data!

That fact is at the heart of what might be the real conclusion of Karaganis and McClure's article: not just that Bloom and Morrison both sort of won the culture wars, but that ultimately they both lost—together with everyone else involved. After all, they point out, what's changed most about the nature of the humanities since the 1980s is the "sharp decline in humanities enrollment." They offer a typical version of quantitative analysis to explain this, suggesting that "the loss of the privileged place accorded to literary expression in society translates into different decisions by students about what to study."

Sure, that's one explanation, but another more plausible one has to do with the fact that the budgets of humanities programs have been dramatically slashed, while the budgets for data-driven projects like Open Syllabus have boomed. Welcome to the logic of Austerity Multiculturalism, which we'll be discussing in much greater detail later in the book: sure, you can have a bigger, better canon, but good luck with that, because we're cutting your budget! In any case, while the Open Syllabus gurus offer some patronizing words of praise for Bloom and Morrison and their ilk, the message is clear: stand down, all you mush-brained literary types; the social scientists—not to mention the data scientists—are now in charge!

Canon Fodder

It's easy to poke fun at the self-seriousness of bespectacled literary types "warring" over how to read William Faulkner or whether to read Alice Walker back in the 1980s. Today, the story of the canon wars is generally retold as one in which both sides foolishly believed "that every time an English teacher put together a reading list, the future of a nation hung in the balance."[9] But

9   Bethany Bryson, *Making Multiculturalism: Boundaries and Meaning in U.S. English Departments* (Palo Alto: Stanford UP, 2005), p. 2.

think back to the role played by The Tradition—or, if you prefer, the Western Canon—in the blood-soaked invention of American monoculture, and that canon's continuing role in sustaining of the myth of white solidarity. After all, literature is one of the ways that a society tells itself the story of who and what it is. So at their most radical, critical engagements with this canon, and with the cultural power they have been accorded, are also attempts to seize hold of this story. Toni Morrison knew the stakes of such work. "Canon building is empire building," was how she summed it up, adding: "Canon defense is national defense."[10]

Morrison's most extended engagement with the bloody business of canons came in a 1988 lecture, "Unspeakable Things Unspoken." The title reflects the mission Morrison undertakes in her talk: "addressing the Afro-American presence in American Literature" in ways "that require neither slaughter nor reification." But she had originally considered another title for her lecture: "Canon Fodder." It wasn't just the pun on "canon" and "cannon" that drew her; it was that the canon wars,

10   Toni Morrison, "Unspeakable Things Unspoken: The Afro-American Presence in American Literature," *Tanner Lectures on Human Values, XI* (Salt Lake City: University of Utah Press, 1990), p. 132.

however genteel the circumstances in which they were being fought, were a life-or-death struggle over a legacy of unspeakable violence. When she placed the words *canon* and *cannon* next to each other, Morrison wrote, "the image became the shape of the cannon wielded on (or by) the body of law. The boom of power announcing an 'officially recognized set of texts.' Cannon defending canon, you might say." And who's the fodder? Morrison is blisteringly clear:

> that host of young men—black or "ethnics" or poor or working-class—who left high school for the war in Vietnam and were perceived . . . as "fodder." Indeed many of those who went, as well as those who returned, were treated as one of that word's definitions: "coarse food for livestock," or, in the context of my thoughts about the subject of this paper, a more applicable definition: "people considered as readily available and of little value." Rude feed to feed the war machine.[11]

Here is one shape of the power wielded by the canon: those not recognized by the "we" created by The Tradition and its keepers can all too easily become fodder for wars at home and abroad, from Vietnam to Iraq to the police-occupied streets of their own cities.

11   Morrison, "Unspeakable Things Unspoken," p. 123.

It's no surprise in this respect that William Bennett, after serving as Ronald Reagan's secretary of education and watchdog of "our Western tradition" at the height of the culture wars, went on to play two other major roles: he was George H. W. Bush's "Drug Czar," presiding over some of the most violent days of the "war on drugs," then subsequently a founding member of the Project for the New American Century, the neoconservative powerbrokers largely credited with masterminding George W. Bush's invasion and occupation of Iraq. If canon defense is national defense, then calling canon defenders like Bennett "culture warriors" goes beyond the metaphorical.

As Morrison and other close and critical readers of "The Western Canon" know, you can find this lesson written into the very heart of The Tradition itself. It's even there, for those willing to look for it, in the work of one William Shakespeare, the son of a glove-maker from the middle of nowhere who ran off to London to become an actor. Although Shakespeare was dismissed as an "upstart crow" by the elitist university wits of his time, he has nevertheless been shoehorned by elitist snobs into a starring role as the brightest, whitest light in The Tradition. But dig a little deeper and he rhymes quite closely with Morrison on how war machines find their fodder. Merrily vicious old Sir John Falstaff, on his way to fight the latest in a series of wars engineered by the nobility in their quest for the English throne, laughingly describes the imminent fate of his piteous-looking company of soldiers to the royal heir, Prince Hal: "Tut, tut, good enough to toss; food for powder, food for powder." It's no wonder: this ragged bunch of poor men are the only ones left once those with means or connections had bribed their way out of fighting the king's glorious war. Falstaff sums up the fate of those condemned to be rude feed for the war machine: "They'll fill a pit as well as better."

The canon, if you read closely enough, is full of cannon fodder.

Ghost in the Machine

That last point is important, since it upends the traditional narrative of the canon wars and their outcome: an institutional multiculturalism whose sole aim is a slightly more "inclusive" canon—The Tradition rebooted, you might say. But that Tradition was originally invented precisely to give a European pedigree to the settler colonial American monoculture. Pretending that this tradition can be stretched a bit so as to make it more "inclusive" is to ignore its foundational monocultural nature. That is, it ignores what Morrison calls "the

whitemale origins and definitions" of The Tradition's
values and belief system.

In "Unspeakable Things Unspoken," Morrison does
demand a space for reading and valuing Afro-American
literature—not through a simple pluralism that applies a
litmus test of "greatness" based on the terms set by whitemale values and definitions, but rather through a fully
transformative process: "the development of a theory of
literature that truly accommodates Afro-American literature: one that is based on its culture, its history, and
the artistic strategies the works employ to negotiate the
world it inhabits."[12] As a model of this transformed theory of literature, much of her lecture is in fact a close
rereading of the traditional (read: "white") canon of
American literature. In other words, far from aiming
to expel all the "dead white men" from the canon,
she invites us to read the work of these writers more
closely—but also more critically.

Her goal in engaging with a canon whose creation
was intended to shore up a monocultural white vision
of "American" identity is to measure the precise dimensions and effects of the "unspeakable things unspoken"
in this canon—the way "American literature," as it had
come to be understood and codified, has violently and

12 Morrison, "Unspeakable Things Unspoken," p. 135.

systematically eliminated Afro-American presence. That presence remains invisible in the American literary canon, but as she reminds us, things that are invisible are not necessarily "not-there": certain absences are so obvious that they call attention to themselves. If you begin to look closely enough, the Afro-American absence becomes a palpable presence, the "ghost in the machine" of the canon. "It only seems that the canon of American literature is 'naturally' or 'inevitably' 'white,'" she writes. "In fact it is studiously so."[13]

This is an incredibly important corrective to contemporary accounts that would reduce the radical work of Morrison and others to simply "expanding" the canon or making it more "inclusive." This is not to say that she isn't invested in adding writers from outside The Tradition to reading lists; of course she is. But at its heart, her project involves fundamentally transforming our whole understanding of that tradition, including its perverse attempt to erase its own relationship to blackness—a perversity multiplied and carried forward by contemporary defenders of the canon.

The power of this transformative criticism is clearest in Morrison's reading of Herman Melville's *Moby Dick*—a canonical novel if there ever was one, although

13   Morrison, "Unspeakable Things Unspoken," p. 139.

it was a critical and commercial flop during its author's lifetime. She re-presents it to us as perhaps the only work of its time that tried to come to terms with the emergence of whiteness as an ideology, in all its bloody horror. Like the white whale itself, whiteness for Melville was "an inhuman idea," a monster intent on "devouring the world as he knew it." For Morrison, both the brilliance and the chaotic disorder of *Moby Dick* stem from Melville's struggle to represent the destructive force of whiteness, at the very moment when it was becoming the defining aspect of American monoculture. In doing so, he declared war on the larger tradition itself, in a way that can't simply be recuperated: "to question the very notion of white progress, the very idea of racial superiority, of whiteness as privileged place in the evolutionary ladder of humankind, and to meditate on the fraudulent, self-destroying philosophy of that superiority . . . that was dangerous, solitary, radical work. Especially then. Especially now."[14]

Revisiting Morrison's radical rereading of a canonical work like *Moby Dick* can have a transformative effect on how we understand the stakes of the literary canon wars. For conservative defenders of the Western canon like the late Harold Bloom, critics of the

14   Morrison, "Unspeakable Things Unspoken," p. 141-44.

canon, whom he bunched together and then dismissed as the "School of Resentment," had no interest in doing a deep reading of the literary texts he revered. Instead, according to Bloom, critics like Morrison were interested only in "destroying all intellectual and aesthetic standards in the humanities and social sciences, in the name of social justice," either by replacing aesthetic criteria with political litmus tests for literary texts or by directly replacing "dead white male" writers with what Bloom called "multicultural bad writing."[15]

But in fact, in her search for the canon's ghost in the machine—the exact shape of the studied absence of Afro-American presence in the creation of American monoculture—Morrison fruitfully expanded and deepened the aesthetic and intellectual standards of literary study. In asserting "its antithesis to blackness" and thereby turning itself "white," canonical American literature committed itself to a set of moves that helped determine its relationship to existing genres, to the nature of the stories it told, and to the aesthetic choices that individual writers made—or that were forced upon them. These are precisely the sorts of questions that

15 Bloom, *The Western Canon*, p. 35; Kenton Robinson, "Foe to Those Who Would Shape Literature to Their Own Ends," *Harford Courant* (October 4, 1994).

literary criticism at its best have always addressed. Some works, like *Moby Dick*, wrestled with the catastrophe produced by whiteness as an ideology and were wrecked in the process, although their explosions were brilliant to behold; others (Morrison mentions the work of Edgar Allan Poe) developed elaborate aesthetic and stylistic devices to circumvent the problem, which had the effect of helping to shape them into something different from what they might have been.

The very character of the "Young American" litera-ture that was at the heart of the development of a white American monoculture, for Morrison, was influenced by the project of making Black presence absent: "In 1850 at the height of slavery and burgeoning abolitionism, American writers chose romance. Where, I wonder, in these romances is the shadow of the presence from which the text has fled?" Bloom and other conservative defenders of the canon claimed that they were the only ones interested in reading and understanding works of "great literature," but Morrison shows us that readers who shriek about how "great literature" transcends pol-itics are the ones really doing violence to literature. To keep the canon intact for the purposes of continuing the monocultural American tradition, and thereby continu-ing the silencing of "the unspeakable things unspoken," she concludes, "is to disenfranchise the writer, diminish the text, and render the bulk of the literature aesthetically and historically incoherent—an exorbitant price for cultural (whitemale) purity, and, I believe, a spendthrift one."[16]

If Herman Melville was on a brave and lonely mission in hurling himself against the horrors of whiteness, how much more so is that the case for Toni Morrison herself. Far from simply pleading for the "inclusion" of the Afro-American tradition made systematically invisible by American monoculture, in "Unspeakable Things Unspoken" and in her subsequent book *Playing in the Dark: Whiteness and the Literary Imagination*, she made a foray right into the heart of the Western Canon itself, and came out with a re-visioned and transformed idea of how this canon needed to be understood. And that's not even to speak of her utterly transformative work as a novelist. It's a perverse tribute to Morrison that her novels—particularly *The Bluest Eye* and *Beloved*—are among the most frequent targets by right-wing mobs eager to ban books that dare to challenge white supremacy. Indeed, Glenn Youngkin's successful racist campaign for governor of Virginia used a campaign ad that called for banning *Beloved* from schools as one of its most

16   Morrison, "Unspeakable Things Unspoken," p. 137, 139.

prominent weapons.[17] Toni Morrison's "dangerous, solitary, radical work" in the canon wars has left its indelible mark, and it is ours to continue. Especially now.

"Official Antiracism": The Latest Phase of Monoculturalism

Morrison doesn't use the term "multiculturalism" in "Unspeakable Things Unspoken," nor do you generally find any mention of the words most associated with today's institutional multiculturalism—diversity, inclusion, equity—in her writing. Her work with literary texts was a move towards transformation, not a request for what she called the "benign coexistence near or within reach of the already sacred texts" offered to "multicultural" texts by the logic of inclusiveness. But the fact that our contemporary account of the canon wars can nevertheless retrospectively include Morrison among those supposedly fighting for "a diversification of the canon" tells us something about the nature of the victory won by institutional multiculturalism. Part of that victory involved minor concessions from the most monoculturalist defenders of the canon. But more

17   See Rebecca Onion, "The Woman Who Wanted *Beloved*
      Banned from Schools Is Right About One Thing," *Slate*
      (October 31, 2021).

significant was institutional multiculturalism's defeat of a radical and truly *critical* multiculturalism, of the sort that can be found in Morrison's literary criticism.

That is, the actual outcome of the canon wars was an uneasy truce between monoculturalist defenders of the Western Canon and liberal (as compared to radical) multiculturalists. The common ground that enabled this truce was a shared willingness to profess a belief in *pluralism* as the fundamental grounding of "American" identity. Conservative defenders of The Tradition used this emphasis on pluralism to insist upon a canon that would be based on assimilation into the traditional American monoculture—the old melting pot model, applied to the literary canon. The liberal multiculturalists, on the other hand, emphasized the need for a more diverse canon that expanded (slightly) to represent America as a mosaic of many cultures—which, at the end of the day, is just a different, slightly more capacious pluralism.

The radical possibility found in Morrison's work, which is also present at a deep level in canonical writers like Melville—the possibility of struggling against the foundational power of whiteness as an ideology at the origins of the United States, and looking with clear eyes upon the horrors committed to instantiate that power, in order to break with that history—had no place in this new form of institutional multicultural-ism. Instead, the history of American monoculturalism was to be dealt with in the same way that corporations today pretend to "confront" white supremacy: via pious slogans. "Mistakes were made, but we will do better going forward."

Institutional multiculturalism has no interest in finding and exorcising the ghost in the machine; it set-tles for murmuring regrets about how canonical writ-ers were "men of their time," but nevertheless founders of a pluralistic nation with the capacity to self-correct. One important effect of an outcome in which neither side ultimately challenged the notion of "America" as a pluralistic society was to uphold the idea of the US as a flawed but perfectible nation. This logic implicitly justified the US in its mission to achieve global hegem-ony and promote its brand of democracy throughout the world—during an era in which the bloody footprints of US imperialism stained the globe, from Latin America to Grenada to Iraq to Somalia.

The institutional multiculturalism that emerged from the end of the literary canon wars sidestepped any real attempt to reckon with the bloody legacy of settler colonial genocide, chattel slavery, or white supremacy. Another way of saying this is that what was ultimately left out of the multicultural canon wars were the anti-racist, anti-capitalist, feminist, queer, and *internationalist* principles that inspired the radical student movements of the 1960s—even though the demands made by those movements were largely responsible for challenging the literary canon in the first place. As a result, once the smoke cleared, "inside the academy, the main result of the canon wars was to enable liberal multiculturalism to defeat critical multiculturalism."[18]

That last phrase comes from Jodi Melamed's important book *Represent and Destroy: Rationalizing Violence in the New Racial Capitalism*, which argues that this moment of truce at the end of the literary canon wars was part of a larger global process. For Melamed, the post-World War II era represented a moment of crisis for a more traditional model of monoculturalism, just at the moment when the US was rising up to assume its new role as "superpower." American monoculturalism needed to be replaced, or at least rebooted. In its place came an "official, state-recognized antiracism."

Don't misunderstand: the production of this "official antiracism" doesn't mean that racism, or for that

18   Jodi Melamed, *Represent and Destroy: Rationalizing Violence in the New Racial Capitalism* (Minneapolis: University of Minnesota Press, 2011), p. 33-34.

matter white supremacy, ended, in the United States or anywhere else, after World War II. Quite the opposite: at home, "official antiracism" covered over the workings of already-existing racism; internationally, it helped support US imperialism all over the globe. In the process, the very term "antiracist" was stripped of the meaning it held for generations of anti-colonial movements. "It should not be possible to be antiracist without being against oppression," Melamed writes. "Yet race-liberal hegemony has been so effective that today in the United States everyone is antiracist, and yet oppression is banal and ubiquitous."[19] Simply put, in the new post-war order, overt racism was bad for business, while a capitalism-friendly and state-approved antiracism (minus the radical politics) was, as they used to say in the 1980s, a winner. The name of this new order is multiculturalism.

The End of Official Anti-Racism: La Lucha Continua

To sum up: by most mainstream accounts, liberal multiculturalists won the culture wars. We can now see what this means: defenders of The Tradition were, to some

19 Melamed, *Represent and Destroy*, p. xi, 49.

extent, vanquished (although they certainly have never surrendered), but what was most soundly defeated was the possibility of a truly critical, insurgent, decolonized and decolonizing multiculturalism.

So here's a takeaway from those wars: a version of liberal multiculturalism won, but more specifically, it was a form of *managerial multiculturalism*. As we'll see in the following chapters, this particular brand of institutional multiculturalism goes hand in hand with the work of *diversity management*, but it also works with and alongside the imposition of direct and deadly violence. Managerial multiculturalism, in other words, proves to be perfectly compatible with the implicit and explicit violence brought to bear against the very student and youth movements that it claims to honor. Meanwhile, a potentially radical version of multiculturalism, one aimed at true decolonization, didn't so much lose as suffer a violent defeat at the hands of the state, corporations, and university administrators. But defeats can be reversed, and that's what this book is ultimately about: reclaiming that legacy of struggle.

And the defenders of The Tradition, those culture warriors fighting for good old American monoculture?

Like horror movie villains, just when you think they're dead, they spring back to life, more malevolent than ever, to wreak further havoc. That word "Again" in "Make America Great Again"? That's precisely the longing for the good old monocultural days.

Chapter Four

KILLING STUDENTS AND
SECURING CAMPUSES, OR CALL
THE MULTICULTURAL POLICE!

In the contemporary context I've been describing in this book so far, it's easy to forget that even the tamest forms of institutional multiculturalism only exist today as the result of radical struggles by social movements, and particularly student movements. To be more specific, the university as we find it today is the product of two opposing forces: on the one hand, radical student movements, particularly movements against racism, capitalism, patriarchy, settler colonialism, and imperialism; on the other hand, the counterinsurgent strategies forged by the state, corporations, and university administrators, which aimed to neutralize the transformative power of these movements.[1] The continuing struggle between those counterforces is, to a great extent, the story I am telling here.

1   For a persuasive and very readable account of this story, see
     Roderick A. Ferguson, *We Demand: The University and Student
     Protests* (Berkeley: U of California P, 2017). I'm indebted to
     Ferguson's book for laying the groundwork for many of the
     arguments that I'll be making in this chapter, and I hope
     readers of this book will seek out *We Demand*, which Ferguson
     dedicates to the ongoing student movements of today.

The administrative cooptation of radical movements under the banner of "multiculturalism" has been
a crucial part of this process. But there's a more explicitly violent side to the story. For this cooptation would
never have been successful if it were not carried out
alongside the much more direct forms of coercion—
including brutal violence—that have been aimed at students over the past fifty years. Sometimes, this violence
has been implicit: for example, via the imposition of
massive student debt and the deliberate impoverishing
of public education via austerity policies. But universities have also been sites of explicit violence. When you
step onto campus grounds, once you get past the multicultural branding, you find yourself, quite literally, in a
militarized space.

The campus police are the iron fist beneath the velvet glove of institutional multiculturalism.

This is the context within which, and against
which, today's student movements operate. One inspiring example of this resistance is the Cops Off Campus
Coalition, a nation-wide "coalition of coalitions" made
up of students and workers at dozens of colleges and
universities organizing to abolish policing on campuses,
from primary and secondary schools to colleges and universities. Cops Off Campus, like many other forms of

abolitionist and anti-racist organizing by students, started in the summer of 2020, driven by the police murders of George Floyd, Breonna Taylor, Tony McDade, and so many others, and by the subsequent popular uprisings against racialized state violence. "Our movement to remove cops from campus," the Cops Off Campus website declares, "comprise one part of these uprisings for Black lives, arguably the largest in US history."

May 2020 will be forever associated with the police murder of George Floyd in Minneapolis, thanks to the popular uprising that arose in the aftermath of this murder and the continuing work of abolitionist organizers, especially youth and student organizers, that has forced an end to the silence around racialized state violence. It's impossible to say what the response would have been like on college campuses that spring and summer if the COVID-19 pandemic hadn't emptied these campuses of students months before the uprisings began. But even under those impossible circumstances, the demand to defund or disband campus police forces, to force universities to offer reparations for their role in slavery, genocide, and segregation, to decolonize the curriculum, and to bring down the symbols of white supremacy resounded on campuses across the United States and around the world.

College administrators, as is their wont, responded to student demands only in order to try to defuse them. Most of the responses were vague: confessions of a need to "do better," to "keep the lines of communication open," and most of all to "listen" and "have conversations" with students whose rage and sorrow could no longer be ignored. Some white male college presidents proved particularly obtuse. The president of Harvard used the occasion to tell students about all the things he believed in, including the Constitution and "the American Dream." The president of Boston University somehow believed that a moment of popular uprising against racialized state violence provided him with a good opportunity to talk about why the "troubled climate" and "divisions in our country" made it really important to bring students back to live on campus in the midst of a surging pandemic. Paul Trible, the president of Christopher Newport University in Virginia, took the tin ear award for tone deafness by using his statement regarding the police murder of George Floyd to complain about property damage in the wake of the murder: more specifically, Trible used his important platform to decry an alleged theft at his son's luxury clothing store. Conspicuously missing from all such statements were words such as "white supremacy," "anti-Black racism," or "Black Lives Matter." Absent altogether were concrete proposals to address structural racism.[2]

Administrative responses to what might have been a truly teachable moment—a moment when colleges and universities could have had a long-delayed conversation about their role in, and responsibility for, the racial and economic inequities laid bare by the pandemic even before the protests began—instead followed an all too familiar pattern. It was all a perfect example of what the *Jezebel* writer Alex Green has dubbed "the Having Conversations Industrial Complex." The endgame of that process is clear: "The Having Conversations Industrial Complex exists to enrich the powerful and defuse radical demands."[3]

Two years later, as this book goes to press, the violent backlash against the radical demands made by student and youth movements in the wake of George Floyd's murder is in full swing. "Cancel culture" is the latest bogeyman of the right, and centrist Democrats, who have been good for nothing but losing elections

2   For all these responses and more, see Lindsay McKenzie, "Words Matter for College Presidents, but So Will Actions," *Inside Higher Education* (June 8, 2020).

3   Alex V. Green, "The Emptiness and Inertia of 'Having Conversations,'" *Jezebel* (July 22, 2020).

since 2014, have decided that if only the "defund the police" movement would go away, all their problems would be over.

Meanwhile, college administrators have put aside their inane statements declaring their opposition to racism—I mean, "racism" is a little too polemical to actually say out loud, but you know what they mean—in order to follow their hearts and do what they do best: act as the handmaidens of austerity. At Penn State, where the athletic director had recently signed a contract worth three-quarters of a million dollars, President Neeli Bendapudi cited budgetary concerns as one reason for canceling a plan to create a Center for Racial Justice—a center which the previous president had promised would serve as "the beginning of the university's efforts towards racial justice and equity."[4] And on many campuses—including the University of Minnesota, a few miles from the site where Derek Chauvin's boot crushed the life from George Floyd—police budgets began, once again, to quietly increase. Despite tireless demands from students to defund the police, as the fall 2021 semester began, UM's president announced that in fact *more*

4   Oyin Adedoyin, "Penn State Scraps Plans for a Racial-Justice Center," *Chronicle of Higher Education* (October 27, 2022).

police would be patrolling, not only on campus, but also in the surrounding neighborhoods.[5]

Back to the Future: May 1970

To understand how we got our current militarized campuses, with institutional multiculturalism providing cover for racist policing, we need to go back exactly fifty years from the month of George Floyd's murder. May 1970 is our starting point, and here too we will encounter state murders of unarmed but supposedly "dangerous" young people. In fact, we'll begin with not one but two state massacres. On May 4, 1970, four Kent State University students protesting against the Vietnam War—Jeffrey Glen Miller, Allison B. Krause, William Knox Schroeder, and Sandra Lee Scheuer— were murdered on campus by National Guard soldiers. Ten days later, city and state police officers in Jackson, Mississippi murdered two Black students—Philip L. Gibbs and James Earl Green—who were protesting against racist violence at Jackson State University, after riddling a women's dorm on campus with more than four hundred bullets.

5   Ryan Faircloth, "University of Minnesota Deploys Safety
     Measures to Quell Crime Near Campus," *Minnesota Star Tribune*
     (September 10, 2021).

There are important differences between these two massacres. The Kent State killings have become part of mainstream historical accounts of "The Sixties." This may be because they are linked to iconic images of students protesting against the Vietnam War: the anti-war protests at Kent State in May 1970 were part of a nationwide wave of student protests following President Richard Nixon's decision to expand the war by invading Cambodia.[6] The timing and nature of the Kent State massacre also makes it a convenient event with which to bookend "The Sixties." Take, for example, the title of the oft-used textbook *From Camelot to Kent State*, first published in 1987, from which many generations of students (me included) have been taught a narrative of "The Sixties" that begins with the euphoria of John F. Kennedy's election and ends with the "tragedy" of Kent State.[7] The moral of the story, I guess, is "expecting too much can get you killed," a good lesson to drum into those of us coming of age in the Reagan-Bush era.

---

6   For a deeper look at the connections between the invasion of Cambodia and the protests at Kent State, see James A. Tyner and Mindy Farmer, *Cambodia and Kent State: In the Aftermath of Nixon's Expansion of the Vietnam War* (Kent, OH: Kent State University Press, 2020).

7   Joan Morrison and Robert K. Morrison, eds., *From Camelot to Kent State: The Sixties Experience in the Words of Those Who Lived It* (New York: Times Books, 1987).

One obvious problem with this narrative is the presentation of the Kent State massacre as a "tragedy," as though the four students were killed by a natural disaster rather than shot in cold blood by US troops occupying their campus.[8] Another problem is that the Jackson State killings, which at the time were closely linked to the state murders at Kent State, have been largely forgotten in these mainstream accounts. It was only fifty years later that the Jackson State massacre came back into the mainstream view, largely because the circumstances resonate so strongly with the massive state violence still being brought to bear against Black protesters and organizers, both on and off campus.[9]

8   For an interesting contemporary account of the killings at Kent State by local journalists—written before the mainstream narrative had come together—see Joe Eszterhas and Michael D. Roberts, *Thirteen Seconds: Confrontation at Kent State* (Cleveland: Gray & Company, 1970). For a more recent analysis that upends many of the conventional understanding of the Kent State Massacre, see Thomas M. Grace, *Kent State: Death and Dissent in the Long Sixties* (Amherst: University of Massachusetts Press, 2016) as well as the documentary *Kent State: The Day the War Came Home* (2000).

9   See Robert Luckett, "Why the Jackson State Massacre Still Matters," *The New York Times* (May 14, 2020). For more on the Jackson State killings as part of a larger wave of violence against Black student organizers—especially, but not only, at historically Black colleges and universities—see Martha Biondi, "Toward a Black University: Radicalism, Repression, and Reform at

Why has Kent State been memorialized and Jackson State forgotten? Let me spell it out: the victims of the Kent State massacre were white; the victims at Jackson State were Black. If you don't believe me, then tell me if you've ever heard about the Orangeburg Massacre. On February 8, 1968, three students from South Carolina State College were murdered and twenty-eight more were injured—most of them shot in the back—by the state police. The students were involved in a peaceful protest against racial segregation in Orangeburg, South Carolina; police officers carrying hunting rifles loaded with buckshot opened fire. The three students who died of their wounds were just eighteen years old. No police officer or city or state official was ever held accountable, but an organizer with the Student Nonviolent Coordinating Committee (SNCC), Cleveland Sellers, who was wounded in the attack, was subsequently arrested and sentenced to a year of hard labor for "inciting to riot."[10] If the massacre at

Historically Black Colleges," in *The Black Revolution on Campus* (Berkeley: University of California Press, 2012).

10   For more on the Orangeburg Massacre, including their historical silencing, see Jack Bass and Jack Nelson, *The Orangeburg Massacre* (Macon, GA: Mercer University Press, 1996) and "Feb. 8, 1968: Orangeburg Massacre," an entry on the *Zinn Education Project* website, along with the 2009 documentary

Jackson State has been largely written out of histories of "The Sixties," that historical forgetting applies even more horrifically to the racist police riot that was the Orangeburg Massacre.

Nixon's "Commission on Campus Unrest" and the Criminalization of Students

So the precedent of unleashing state violence—and specifically racialized violence—against student protesters certainly didn't begin with Kent State and Jackson State. Nevertheless, those two weeks in May 1970 mark a turning point in the development of today's militarized university. In particular, the aftermath of the Jackson State and Kent State killings led to the development of two forms of institutional coercion—one subtle and covert, the other violent and overt—that we would all recognize today: the rhetorical commitment to multicultural diversity by university administrations, and the simultaneous militarizing of university campuses through the creation and augmentation of heavily armed campus police forces.

A key element in this process was President Nixon's "Commission on Campus Unrest," established

Scarred Justice: The Orangeburg Massacre 1968, directed by Bestor Cram and Judy Richardson.

a few weeks after the Kent State and Jackson State killings. Ostensibly set up in response to these "great tragedies," the commission's report rewrote the story so that student protesters were themselves the *source* of violence—erasing, in the process, the fact that students had in fact been the *victims* of massive and murderous state violence. The rhetoric of the Commission's report could just as easily be used today by an establishment politician (from either party): "There can be no more trashing, no more rock-throwing, no more arson, no more bombing by protesters. No grievance, philosophy, or political idea can justify the destruction and killing we have witnessed."[11]

In the Commission's version of reality, nonviolent student protests immediately become equated with acts of property destruction (including the vague accusation of "trashing"), which are directly attributed to protesters; on the other hand, the passive voice comes into play when it comes to the "killing we have witnessed." No one actually did the killing, it seems (certainly not the state!); it just happened, as the inevitable outcome of those disruptive protests. In effect, the protesters unleashed

11   *The Report of the President's Commission on Campus Unrest* (Washington, DC: U.S. Department of Health, Education, and Welfare, 1970), p. 2, quoted in Ferguson, *We Demand*, p. 18.

the violence that killed them; the students, it appears, killed themselves. That sleight of hand is still in play fifty years later.[12]

The aftermath of the murders at Kent State and Jackson State clearly marks the emergence of on-campus police departments that are now all but mandatory at both public and private universities. When Nixon's Commission on Campus Unrest issued its report in 1970, universities by and large did not have their own police forces. Today, thanks to lobbying by US college presidents and the work of local, state, and federal legislators, virtually all public universities, and more than 90 percent of private universities, have their own police departments. Most of these university police departments allow campus officers to carry guns and to patrol

12 A whole book could be written about the use of the passive voice to avoid holding states accountable for their violence. I've written further about this in the case of mainstream reporting about Palestine; see "Palestine in Scare Quotes: From the NYT Grammar Book," *Jadaliyya* (July 12, 2011). One example: in 2010, Israeli Defense Forces shot and killed protesters who were part of a Turkish flotilla attempting to deliver humanitarian aid to blockaded Gaza. *The New York Times* neatly deployed the passive voice in reporting this act of direct state violence: "nine people died in May in Israel's raid on a Turkish flotilla." What happened on the flotilla? "Nine people died." Or as Philip Weiss rephrased it, with savage irony, "They up and died!" (Philip Weiss, "They Up and Died!" *Mondoweiss* [October 14, 2010]).

and arrest not just on campus but also in off-campus communities.[13]

When I first encountered that fact that campus police had really only existed since the 1970s while reading Roderick Ferguson's book *We Demand: The University and Student Protests*, it was a startling revelation. Having gone to college and then graduate school in the 1980s and 1990s, the campus police seemed to me as much an eternal presence as the library and the cafeteria. It was sobering to learn that the omnipresence of police on campus had begun barely a decade before I started college. Once the process was set in motion, however, it didn't take much to convince state legislatures that students needed to be policed. In fact, in 2020, a Massachusetts Democratic state senator introduced a bill that would *require* campus police officers at any state college, community college, or public university to be issued firearms—even if the college administration or the campus community doesn't want armed cops on their campus.[14]

13   Libby Nelson, "Why Nearly All Colleges Have an Armed Police Force," *Vox* (July 29, 2015); Angela Wright, "How Armed Police Officers on Campus Have Become a Ubiquitous Part of American College Life," *MacLean's* (June 25, 2020).

14   Matt Murphy, "Bill Zeroes in on Arming MassArt Campus Police, Despite Resistance from the College's Leaders," WBUR report (January 31, 2020).

Unquestionably, the move to set up armed police forces at colleges and universities was a direct response to the student movements of the 1960s and the work these movements did to open up universities to communities that had previously been excluded. Put plainly, the fight to desegregate public education led the state to put cops on campus. Nixon's Commission on Campus Unrest (which included both college presidents and police chiefs) declared as much, recommending the formation of campus police forces as the key to fighting "disruption" on campuses: "A fully staffed and trained campus police force at its best can perform the functions of a small municipal police department with respect to campus disorders."[15]

Decolonization is an agenda for total disorder. No wonder that when student movements fought to decolonize their universities, the state called the cops.

"Homeland Security Football Missions" and Other Military-Grade Emergencies

When I talk about the unleashing of explicit violence against students and their communities by campus police forces, I'm not being metaphorical. The past decade

15 *Report of the President's Commission on Campus Unrest*, p. 132, quoted in Ferguson, *We Demand*, p. 29.

alone has seen fatal shootings by campus police officers at San Jose University, the University of the Incarnate Word in San Antonio, Portland State University, Florida Institute of Technology, and Georgia Tech, where a twenty-one-year-old student activist who was the president of the college's Pride Alliance was shot and killed by campus police while the student was suffering from a period of distress due to mental illness. This is in addition to thousands of other reports of police violence (particularly against students of color) and, as of 2017, over 52,000 arrests per year made by campus police.[16] One of the few instances in which deadly violence carried out by campus police gained national attention occurred in 2015, when University of Cincinnati police officer Ray Tensing shot Samuel DuBose in the back, killing the forty-three-year old Black man, during a traffic stop that occurred off campus. Fact: over 80 percent of campus police forces have the power to patrol

16   See Nelson, "Why Nearly All Colleges"; Meerah Powell, "Bill Introduced to Disarm Campus Police At 2 Oregon Universities," *OPB* (Feburary 28, 2019); Cobretti D. Williams, "Race and Policing in Higher Education," *The Activist History Review* (November 19, 2019); Yunkyo Kim and Megan Munce, "Students Call on University to Divest from Police Forces and Invest in Black Communities," *The Daily Northwestern* (June 10, 2020).

and arrest—and, apparently, to shoot people to death—outside campus boundaries.

Two other well-documented incidents occurred within days of each other in April 2019: Stephanie Washington, an unarmed Black woman, was shot in the face while sitting in her parked car in New Haven by a Yale University police officer (about a mile from campus); and, in an incident captured on video that went viral, Alexander McNab, a Black senior at Columbia University, was violently pinned against a counter in the Barnard College library by campus police officers who had asked him, without any particular cause, to show them his student ID (a request that had not been made of any other students entering the building).[17]

In such cases, even when deadly violence is used against students or members of the community, campus police officers are rarely held accountable. The case of

17 See Eric Levenson, "Body Camera Footage Shows Moments Police Opened Fire in Controversial Yale Shooting," CNN (April 24, 2019); Sharon Otterman, "Black Columbia Student's Confrontation with Security Becomes Flashpoint Over Racism on Campus," *The New York Times* (April 18, 2019). For more on the Yale case and its relationship to the university's ongoing predatory relationship to the Black community in New Haven, see Davarian L. Baldwin, *In the Shadow of the Ivory Tower: How Universities are Plundering Our Cities* (New York: Bold Type Books, 2021).

Ray Tensing is particularly indicative of the extent to which university administrations are beholden to their police departments. After being charged with the murder of Samuel DuBose ("This office has probably reviewed upward of 100 police shootings," the county prosecutor declared at the time, "and this is the first time where we thought this is without question a murder"), Tensing was fired by the university and subsequently tried twice, but neither jury could reach a unanimous verdict and both cases ended in mistrials. Ultimately, Tensing was awarded $344,000 in back pay and legal fees by the University of Cincinnati after filing a contractual grievance to protest his "wrongful termination."[18] In doing so, the university administration implicitly admitted the reality that now holds on college campuses: shooting and killing an unarmed Black man, in the back, for the crime of having an incorrectly attached license plate on this car, should not be considered a valid reason for a campus police officer to lose his job.

To sum it up: fifty years on from the killings at Jackson State and Kent State, the militarization of

18   German Lopez, "Samuel DuBose: What We Know About the University of Cincinnati Police Shooting," *Vox* (July 30, 2015); "University of Cincinnati Paying Ray Tensing More than $300K in Back Pay, Legal Fees," WCPO-Cincinnati (May 22, 2018).

campuses has reached an unprecedented level. Using the word "militarized" is no rhetorical gesture: a little-known federal initiative, with the sinister name "the 1033 program," allows the transfer of surplus Defense Department equipment to federal, state, and local law enforcement agencies, including colleges, universities, and K-12 police departments. Since 1990, more than one hundred colleges and universities have received military supplies through the program, including semi-automatic rifles, armored vehicles, camouflage Humvees, and even "mine-resistant ambush protected vehicles (MRAPs)"—Ohio State University has one that it brings out for football games, citing the need for "homeland security football missions." When, thanks to student demands, the University of Maryland finally agreed to divest from the 1033 program in July 2020, the equipment that it returned or sold included fifty M16 semiautomatic rifles, an armored truck, three hundred magazine cartridges, seventy-nine gun sights, two camouflage Humvees, and an armored vehicle that campus police had nicknamed "The Peacekeeper."[19]

19 Sara Weissman, "Over 100 Campus Police Departments Got Military Equipment Through This Federal Program," *Diverse: Issues in Higher Education* (July 20, 2020); Victoria Chamberlin, "As Federal Programs Continue to Militarize Campus Cops, Some Universities Reconsider," *Guns & America* (July 9, 2020).

If campus police are literally military forces, what does that say about the university's relationship to those it claims to serve, particularly its students and workers, or to the larger communities in which it is located? The answer can be found in Angela Davis' analysis of the brutal response to protests following the police murder of Michael Brown in Ferguson, Missouri in 2014. The overwhelmingly violent police response to largely nonviolent protests in Ferguson, Davis notes, dramatically revealed the extent to which the police had become a fully militarized force. Images of police in armored vehicles, carrying assault rifles, wearing camouflage uniforms and night-vision googles and firing rubber bullets, stun grenades, and tear gas grenades at unarmed protesters (and journalists) in Ferguson circulated widely. Clearly, all this military hardware had already been on hand; the cops were just waiting for a reason to bring it out of storage.

But this revelation of the full extent of police militarization in turn demands a different understanding of the situation on the ground. Police officers, in theory at least, are there to "protect and serve" members of the community, but occupying soldiers are simply trained to shoot to kill. "We saw the way in which that manifested itself in Ferguson," Davis concludes.[20] The military analogy goes a step further, since what Davis calls the "global context" of the Ferguson protests also applies to campus police forces:

> What we saw in the police reaction to the resistance . . . revealed the extent to which local police departments have been equipped with military arms, military technology, military training. The militarization of the police leads us to think about Israel and the militarization of the police there—if only the images of the police and not of the demonstrators had been shown, one might have assumed that Ferguson was Gaza.[21]

Campus police have been part of this internationalized security apparatus that has increasingly linked law enforcement in the US and Israel. Police departments from the Universities of Texas Southwestern, Vermont, and Wisconsin-Madison have all sent delegations to Israel to study "counter-terrorism" methods. So have police departments from at least four universities in Georgia,

20 Angela Davis, "Ferguson Reminds Us of the Importance of a Global Context," *Freedom Is a Constant Struggle: Ferguson, Palestine, and the Foundations of a Movement* (Chicago: Haymarket Books, 2015), p. 14.

21 Davis, "Ferguson Reminds Us of the Importance of a Global Context," p. 14-15.

thanks to the Georgia International Law Enforcement Exchange (GILEE), a joint program co-sponsored by Georgia State University and local law enforcement.

As is so often the case, if you scratch the surface of what seems to be a local struggle, you almost immediately discover international connections. In the case of Ferguson, the international connections exposed by militarized policing had their dialectical reflection in the inspiring connections established between student and youth movements resisting racialized violence in the US and in Palestine. As police unleashed their attacks upon protesters in Ferguson, young Palestinian activists who have had all too many experiences with tear gas wielded by Israeli soldiers offered practical advice via social media. The connections went a step further: as activists in both places noted, the same tear gas cannisters (manufactured by a US company) were being used in both places. The subsequent and ongoing solidarity between liberation movements in the US and Palestine—marked by, among many other examples, the 2015 *Black Solidarity Statement with Palestine* signed by more than 1,000 individuals and 39 organizations, and the strong shows of solidarity from organizations involved in the Movement for Black Lives during the most recent Israeli massacre in Gaza in May 2021—shows that the global connections that manifest themselves in campus policing find their counterpart in the internationalism of youth movements that continue to struggle for decolonization.

The Wars Come Home

Moving back fifty years, from May 2020 to May 1970, helps us to historicize today's racialized and militarized campus policing. But there's one important stop we need to make for the story to be complete: September 2001. The 9/11 attacks, and the subsequent (still ongoing) global War on Terror carried out by the US and its allies, has unleashed untold horrors throughout the world. While the militarization of the police, including campus police, certainly didn't begin in 2001, the logic of the War on Terror fundamentally changed the nature of domestic policing. At a more directly material level, much of the military equipment that campus police now deploy flowed directly to them as part of the War on Terror logic—that's how Ohio State wound up with a combat-ready military vehicle for their "homeland security football missions." This was also the period during which state, local, and university police officers started attending "counterterrorism" trainings in other countries, particularly Israel. It shouldn't be surprising, then, that Palestine solidarity organizing, especially the tireless work of student activists belonging to Students for Justice in Palestine chapters on campuses throughout the country, has been systematically repressed.[22]

Another post-9/11 effect on domestic policing was the formation of the Departments of Homeland Security (DHS) and Immigration and Customs Enforcement (ICE), and the development of "intelligence-led policing" tactics by federal, state, and local police forces, including campus police. This included pervasive surveillance of "suspicious" communities—which were, of course, overwhelmingly communities of color. On

22   For more background on the War on Terror and the militarization of the police, see Jessica Katzenstein's excellent report *The Wars Are Here: How the United States' Post-9/11 Wars Helped Militarize U.S. Police*, "Costs of War" Project, Watson Institute for International and Public Affairs, Brown University (September 16, 2020) (available online). For more on the training of US police forces in Israel, see Alice Speri, "Israel Security Forces Are Training American Cops Despite History of Rights Abuses," *The Intercept* (September 15, 2017). For a chilling account of the repression of Palestine solidarity organizing on campus, see *The Palestine Exception to Free Speech: A Movement Under Attack in the US*, published by Palestine Legal and the Center for Constitutional Rights, in 2015, as well as the yearly reports published by Palestine Legal since then. And for an excellent account of the steadfastness of Palestine solidarity organizing by students in the face of this repression, see Nora Barrows-Friedman, *In Our Power: U.S. Students Organize for Justice in Palestine* (Washington, DC: Just World Books, 2014).

university campuses, the violence of these surveillance policies has been visited most dramatically upon Arab, Muslim, and South Asian students and communities. One example was the "special registration" program set up in September 2002 by the Immigration and Naturalization Service (INS), which required "non-immigrant aliens," including international students, from a specified list of countries to "voluntarily" register themselves. The racist nature of the program was transparently obvious: initially, the program targeted nationals from Iran, Iraq, Libya, Sudan, and Syria; ultimately, a total of twenty-five countries were listed, all of them either located in the Middle East or North Africa or Muslim-majority nations, with one stark exception that proved the rule: North Korea.

There has been a great national forgetting of the horror of special registration, but the toll taken upon communities was staggering: when it was first enforced in southern California, for example, hundreds of registrants, mostly Iranians, were arrested or detained; people seeking to voluntarily comply with the new rules were handcuffed, sometimes leg-ironed and transported to jails for visa violations, and suffered verbal abuse, sleep deprivation, and body cavity searches. Huge numbers of people throughout the US were detained, and many were ultimately deported (while an uncountable number, to use a repellent euphemism, "self-deported"). Within months, the implementation of "special registration" had resulted in the removal of more Arabs and Muslims from the US than the total number of foreign nationals deported in the infamous red-baiting Palmer raids of 1919.[23] I hadn't yet started teaching at Kingsborough, but a colleague later told me that soon after 9/11, huge numbers of students from neighboring communities—particularly Arab, Bangladeshi, and Pakistani communities—simply disappeared from campus after special registration began. A student who was enrolled in one of Kingsborough's English as a Second Language programs at the time told me years later about being pulled out of class along with a few other students to be interrogated about their immigration status. All the students were Muslim.

Beyond the particular horrors of special registration, state surveillance and public vilification of Arab, Muslim, and South Asian communities had significant effects on campus. For example: soon after 9/11, the New York City Police Department established a secret surveillance program that has mapped, monitored, and analyzed American Muslim daily life throughout

23   Louise Cainkar, "Targeting Muslims, at Ashcroft's Discretion," *Middle East Report* (March 14, 2003).

the city and its surrounding states. One important target of this surveillance were colleges and universities, particularly students who belonged to Muslim Student Associations (MSA) or related groups. CUNY was a particular target. After "mapping" thirty-one MSAs in New York, the NYPD program came to focus on seven that it listed as "of concern"; six of the seven were part of the CUNY system. Among the reasons for targeting MSAs were their choice of speakers, organizing "militant paintball trips," or simply the claim that some members were "politically active." Police monitored students' emails and online activity on a daily basis. When student organizations invited speakers to campus, the NYPD recorded the speakers' backgrounds, countries of origins, political beliefs, and even the names of students who posted events online.[24]

After operating secretly for a decade, the NYPD's surveillance program was finally exposed thanks to a series of articles published in 2011. But even the public exposure of the program's existence didn't stop the surveillance of Muslim students at CUNY. Arguably

24 Diala Shamas and Nermeen Arastu, *Mapping Muslims: NYPD Spying and Its Impact on American Muslims* (New York: Muslim American Civil Liberties Coalition (MACLC) and Creating Law Enforcement Accountability & Responsibility (CLEAR) Project, 2013), p. 39-40.

the most egregious case occurred at Brooklyn College, where an undercover NYPD officer posed as a young woman named "Mel" who was supposedly seeking to convert to Islam. Beginning in the spring of 2011, "Mel" systematically infiltrated student life at the college, becoming a fixture at MSA events and activities, befriending many young Muslim women and working her way into their lives on and off campus (she was even a bridesmaid in one student's wedding), inquiring about their politics, participating in clubs, and joining numerous listservs, particularly those involving political organizing. Notably, when students of color sought to form a unity coalition to bring together student organizations on campus (including Black, Hispanic, and Muslim groups, as well as Students for Justice in Palestine) in 2014, around the time of the protests in Ferguson, "Mel" attended their initial meetings. She was finally exposed when she testified in a separate court case; students at Brooklyn College recognized her picture online, realizing with horror that someone who had been in their lives for four years was in fact an undercover cop.[25]

25   The report of undercover police surveillance of Muslim students at Brooklyn College was first broken by the *Gothamist* in 2015: see Aviva Stahl, "NYPD Undercover 'Converted' to Islam to Spy on Brooklyn College Students," *Gothamist* (October 29, 2015) and "Brooklyn College Students: NYPD Illegally Spied on Us and Lied About It," *Gothamist* (January 5, 2016).

But students belong to MSAs, and Muslim students more generally, had been overtaken with suspicion long before that. Indeed, fostering a climate of suspicion is one of the aims of undercover policing, which is why its revelation can actually increase its power—if members of a community or organization find out that they are being surveilled, that means *anyone* could be a cop. Couple the omnipresence of heavily armed police officers with the ever-present possibility that the person sitting next to you in class or in a meeting might be an undercover cop, and you begin to understand the deeply hostile climate facing student activists—particular Arab, Muslim, and South Asian students—at a place like Brooklyn College. As the 2013 report *Mapping Muslims: NYPD Spying and Its Impact on American Muslims* concludes: "The repercussions of surveillance on student life are significant: students we have spoken with showed that awareness of surveillance affected the sorts of events that they host, the discussions

Jeanne Theoharis, a Distinguished Professor of Political Science at Brooklyn College and an advisor to several students who were under surveillance, subsequently wrote an extended piece about the case, which in turn inspired the filmmakers Katie Mitchell and Danielle Varga to create a short film, *Watched*, that movingly records the effects of surveillance on two Brooklyn College students. See Jeanne Theoharis, "'I Feel Like a Despised Insect': Coming of Age Under Surveillance in New York," *The Intercept* (February 18, 2016) and *Watched*, dir. Katie Mitchell and Danielle Varga (Collective Eye Films, 2018).

they have, the spaces they occupy, their academic development, civic engagement, and even leadership choices."[26]

Not surprisingly, many Muslim students subsequently avoided anything that could be perceived as "political" activities on campus. At Brooklyn College, the MSA, which had previously been part of coalitions with other student groups (including Students for Justice in Palestine), posted a sign asking members to refrain from having any political conversations in the MSA's club space. In this, it followed the lead of other MSAs who banned political discussions—after all, students quite reasonably concluded that any such discussions would be monitored and could only be used against them.

Muslim students even limited their expression of political beliefs during class discussions or in their academic writing. One Brooklyn College student described asking a friend who was a civil rights lawyer to read over her papers before she handed them in: "Anything that has to do with criticizing the Iraq war, Hamas, I've been thinking about writing about the National Defense Authorization Act—I wonder whether I should even do it. Cyrus said write about it, but then if the teachers were ever asked, they'll have to produce that document. And you don't know what's going to be cut and pasted from that." Another CUNY

26   Shamas and Arastu, *Mapping Muslims*, p. 39.

student, summing up the climate and the consequences of police surveillance on campus, concluded: "I don't want to be sitting at a roundtable, I'll just be wondering whether someone will be secretly taking notes and sending it God knows where. They would write 'that girl thinks this'—then whose door are they going to knock on?"[27]

You may be thinking: this is all shocking stuff, but surely these are the sorts of bad, violent, racist things that any good multiculturalist would be *against*? Well, CUNY administrators, who are very happy to advertise themselves as the multiculti promoters of "diversity university," claimed ignorance of the NYPD surveillance program, despite the fact that a Memorandum of Agreement specifies that NYPD personnel can only enter CUNY campuses "upon the request or approval of a CUNY official." No CUNY administrator has ever openly criticized the NYPD surveillance program or offered any substantive apology or reparations to students targeted by the cops.[28] In fact, all too often we find ostensibly multiculturalist administrators marching onto the field of battle alongside—well, more often, behind—the police.

27 Shamas and Arastu, *Mapping Muslims*, p. 43-44.

28 Conor Skelding, "CUNY: 'No Knowledge' of Undercover NYPD Targeting Muslims on Campus," *Politico* (November 24, 2015).

Chapter Five

MULTICULTURALISM AND DIVERSITY, OR THE DIFFERENCE THAT MAKES NO DIFFERENCE

The Multicultural Center was established in 1989 following student protest. [In] 1988, students belonging to the student group CARE (Coalition Against Racist Education) took over Jenness House—the temporary home of the Dean's Office . . . . Among the 15 demands the students asked for were a) more minority faculty to be hired, b) better recruitment of ethnic-minority students from low income backgrounds, c) for all students to be required to take a course focusing on the minority experience, and d) for the college to establish a Multicultural Center . . . . The college immediately began to work on establishing a Multicultural Center.[1]

The Colorblind Rainbow Center for Campus Diversity was begrudgingly founded in 2015 after 25 students occupied the Dean's Office suite and broke our communal Keurig . . . . The CRCCD shares the House with staff and faculty of the African American, Caribbean, Latinx, East Asian, Gender/Sexuality, and Jewish Studies Programs. The Director also shares the responsibility for partnering with these programs to conduct receptions, lectures, workshops, food festivals, and non-confrontational parades in support of all historically excluded populations. The community-wide commitment to an inclusive, equitable campus is on your shoulders.[2]

One of these quotes is real, one is parody. Which is which? I realize it's a bit hard to tell. The first passage comes from the website of the Davis Multicultural

1   "History of the Davis Center," from the Williams College website.

2   Tatiana McInnis and Amanda Lehr, "The Colorblind Rainbow Center for Campus Diversity Seeks a New Director to Tell Us That Nothing Is Wrong," *McSweeney's Internet Tendency* (July 8, 2020).

Center, located at the real (and really wealthy) Williams College. The second is from a satirical account of the Colorblind Rainbow Center for Campus Diversity, located at the fictional College University. "The Colorblind Rainbow Center for Campus Diversity Seeks a New Director to Tell Us That Nothing Is Wrong," published by *McSweeney's Internet Tendency*, is a brilliant send-up of the institutional absurdity embodied by such multicultural centers in the neo-liberal university. In fact, the co-writer of the piece previously served as Associate Director of the Davis Multicultural Center, until the Williams College administration made what they described as "structural changes" to the Center's leadership (including install-ing an Assistant Vice President as its director). We can therefore assume that any resemblance to actual places, events, and persons (living or dead) is clearly *not* coincidental.

The *McSweeney's* article takes the form of a fake job ad, but at the time it was published, Williams College really was looking for a new director for its multicultural center; most of the previous staff had left to protest those "structural changes" imposed by the administration.[3]

3   See Haley Bossé, William Ren, darien k n manning, Claudia Inglessis, Louisa Belk, Michael Nettesheim, and Sareena

The fictional Rainbow Center is located in the basement of the Jefferson Davis Building—a bit of dark humor that's all too plausible, since for decades there have been campuses named for Davis and other Confederate figures in Mississippi and Alabama (although some of their names were finally changed during the statue-toppling summer of 2020). Meanwhile, Williams' actual multicultural center is named for W. Allison Davis, a Williams alum who was refused a teaching job at the college in 1925 because he was Black. Naming the Center after Davis is clearly the college's attempt at a mea culpa, but when it comes to faculty hiring at Williams, Jefferson Davis would still approve: according to current stats, the Williams College faculty is more than 85 percent white; less than 4 percent of the faculty is Black or African American. Even though the lead demand of student protesters in 1988 was for more diverse faculty to be hired, the number of Black faculty at the college today is basically identical to what it was at that time.

Judging from the real-life job listing posted on Williams College's website, the duties of any would-be Director of the Davis Center seem by definition impossibly broad. They include "fostering opportunities

Khanal, "Why We Left the Davis Center: Systemic Neglect and Structural Changes," *The Williams Record* (February 26, 2020).

for students, faculty and staff to engage in productive discourse around issues of difference and belonging, including race, ethnicity, class, gender, sexual orientation, nationality, religion and spirituality, and their intersectionalities." In much the same spirit of convivial yet encyclopedic vagueness, the Rainbow Center's satirical job listing specifies that "the person who fills this role must plan to join every committee, task force, discussion group, coffee break, and secret meeting on campus to keep tabs on those who seek actionable change." The seeming omnipotence of such a position, and the rhetorical importance that universities give to multiculturalism more generally, is directly contradicted by the actual experience of those who have held these sorts of jobs, whether at universities, or in primary or secondary schools, or in corporations or nonprofits, or really any place where what has come to be called institutional "diversity work" happens.

The feminist scholar Sara Ahmed has been particularly brilliant at documenting the gap between the empty rhetoric that institutions use to describe their commitment to "diversity" versus what actually goes on at these institutions. Thanks to the passage of the Race Relations Amendment Act by Parliament in 2000, all public organizations in the UK are now required by law to implement a "race equality policy and action plan." But the sense of seriousness that this implies is definitely not reflected in the workings of these same public organizations. As one diversity practitioner put it in an interview with Ahmed, "she only had to open her mouth in meetings to witness eyes rolling as if to say, 'Oh, here she goes.'" "It was from experiences like this," Ahmed adds, "that I developed an equation: rolling eyes = feminist pedagogy."[4] It's not for nothing that Ahmed's brilliant blog is called Feminist Killjoys.

Those who are made to embody this eye-roll-inducing work of representing and thus enforcing multiculturalism in institutions are, we're told by the leaders of these institutions, extraordinarily influential, and their work extremely valuable. "The Director of the Davis Center will lead inclusion efforts at the college," Williams College's job description intones. But in reality, as another interviewee told Ahmed, the actual role she performed, as both representative and embodiment of multicultural diversity, was in fact that of a mascot:

4   Sara Ahmed, *What's the Use? On the Uses of Use* (Durham: Duke University Press, 2019), p. 173-74.

"If you are a mascot you are silent, everything you amount to is nothing, you are stuffing, if that, a skeleton with stuffing. I was kept out of the frame of the management structure; I had no control over how the money was spent, who was being employed, who was being invited to the advisory board. I was effectively silenced." You are stuffing; a skeleton with stuffing. . . . What happens when the stuffing speaks? What happens when those who embody diversity theorize for ourselves? She told me what happens. She documented seventy-two instances of racial and sexual harassment directed toward her because she refused to be silent.[5]

Ahmed first started writing about the experiences of those "in charge of" institutional multi-culturalism and diversity after she was asked to serve on a committee that wrote her university's new race equality policy in 2000. "So we wrote the document," Ahmed noted a few years later, "and the university, along with many others, was praised for its policy, and the Vice-Chancellor was able to congratulate the university on its performance: we did well. *A document that documented the racism of the university became usable as a measure of good performance.*"[6]

5   Ahmed, *What's the Use?* p. 189.

6   Sara Ahmed, "Declarations of Whiteness: The Non-Performativity of Anti-Racism," *Borderlands* 3.2 (2004).

The incredulous, outraged italics in that last sentence belong to Ahmed, though I certainly share the feeling.

In 2016, Sara Ahmed resigned her position as Professor of Race and Cultural Studies at the University of London to protest the institution's utter failure to address the pervasive sexual harassment of students. "I have resigned," she wrote in May 2016, "because the costs of doing this work have been too high." In "Resignation Is a Feminist Issue," she expanded on this: "What if our own work of exposing a problem is used as evidence there is no problem? Then you have to ask yourself: can I keep working here? What if staying employed by an institution means you have to agree to remain silent about what might damage its reputation?"[7] Indeed—the Colorblind Rainbow Center for Campus Diversity seeks a new director to tell us that nothing is wrong.

That *McSweeney's* article is brilliant and hilarious, in a laugh-cry sort of way. But it's hard to really call it *satire*; we've reached the point where the work of multicultural diversity management at universities and other institutions has become so shameless and cynical that it inadvertently satirizes itself. As film critic Anthony Lane

7   Sara Ahmed, "Resignation" (May 30, 2016) and "Resignation Is a Feminist Issue" (August 27, 2016), *Feminist Killjoy*.

complained of the Will Ferrell movie *Eurovision Song Contest*, "That which already lies beyond parody is, by definition, impossible to lampoon."

The Difference That Makes No Difference: Diversity to the Rescue

To find a way into this situation, we need to look more closely at the last word in The Colorblind Rainbow Center's title: *diversity*. As we saw in chapter three, the "American" intellectual tradition has been one of monoculturalism, broadly speaking. Within the contemporary university, the word generally deployed against this sort of monoculturalism is *diversity*. Like multiculturalism more generally, diversity efforts carried out by today's neoliberal universities only exist due to the struggles of decades past. In fact, today the terms *multiculturalism* and *diversity* tend to keep company together when colleges and universities describe their mission, course offerings, and general philosophy.

For example, if you Google "university multicultural diversity," you'll find a plethora of nearly identical mission statements. One of the first you are likely to encounter is the "Multicultural Diversity" statement found on the website of Corban University, a private evangelical school in Salem, Oregon, where the student body is 75 percent white and the faculty 85 percent white. Nevertheless, "At Corban University," the statement begins, "we value multicultural diversity." If you were to peruse the website of pretty much any college or university, I dare say you would find some version of this statement expressing a commitment to "multicultural diversity" (and, very likely, similar demographics, especially when it comes to the whiteness of the faculty). As with Corban, though, you might be hard-pressed to find this commitment reflected in the demographics of the actual people who study and teach there, or in any structural or material efforts to understand and change this misfit between rhetoric and demographic reality. Daniel McNeil, a keen observer of multiculturalist rhetoric in Canada, has coined the useful phrase "multicultural snake oil" for such meaningless sentiments.[8]

For administrative convenience, "multiculturalism" and "diversity" tend to be more or less interchangeable. When some level of differentiation is called for, it is usually addressed as a question of emphasis. *Diversity*, we're told, emphasizes, acknowledges, and ultimately respects differences as differences, without valuing some differences more than others. *Multiculturalism*, by

8   Daniel McNeil, "Wrestling with Multicultural Snake Oil:
     A Newcomer's Introduction to Black Canada," *Unsettling the
     Great White North: Black Canadian History*, eds. Michele A.
     Johnson and Funké Aladejebi (Toronto: University of Toronto
     Press, 2021).

contrast, emphasizes inclusiveness and embraces difference as the impetus towards creating a new kind of group identity. This understanding of the distinction between the two terms—diversity as emphasizing (and valuing) difference, multiculturalism as emphasizing (and valuing) inclusivity—has been worked out mostly explicitly by the political philosopher Will Kymlicka. His articulation of "multicultural democracy" provides an example: "A comprehensive theory of justice in a multicultural state will include both universal rights, assigned to individuals regardless of group membership, and certain group-differentiated rights or 'special status' for minority cultures."[9] A multicultural democracy, in other words, doesn't seek to simply absorb or obliterate "minority cultures" but still has its basis in "universal" categories like citizenship and human rights, so long as those categories are sufficiently inclusive.

Of course, the term "minority cultures" here still implies a "majority" monoculture at the center—and surprise, it turns out to be Euro-American culture! So this leaves us mired in the same old problem: Kymlicka's "multicultural democracy" still implicitly (and sometimes explicitly) locates Europe as the center

9   Will Kymlicka, *Multicultural Citizenship: A Liberal Theory of Minority Rights* (Oxford: Clarendon Press, 1996), p. 6.

and sees everybody else—that is, most of the world—as "minority cultures."

In some activist circles, the sort of distinction drawn between the two terms makes multiculturalism, with its emphasis on creating a different form of group identity and its orientation towards the future, preferable to diversity, which according to this account doesn't move beyond a bland respect for the other as other. A blog post written by a self-described white male social justice activist lays out this argument. He describes a training focused on racial and cultural issues whose Black female facilitator asked the mostly white participants to stop using the term "diversity." In a culture built on white privilege, she explains, "Diversity becomes a conversation about those people who are different by those who consider themselves 'normal.'" By contrast, the facilitator argued, "multiculturalism" begins from "the acknowledgment that we all belong to human communities that are made up of many cultures, perspectives, orientations, formations, and life experiences."[10]

This makes a certain kind of sense. But so too does the opposite argument. Shirley Steinberg, in her introduction to the collection *Diversity and Multiculturalism:*

10 Bob Patrick, "Diversity and Multiculturalism," *The Inclusive Latin Classroom* (May 5, 2019).

A Reader, notes that she hadn't originally intended to include the word "multiculturalism" in the title. Putting diversity first is part of what she describes, from within the field of education, as an effort to "turn to diversity as a more inclusive and critical term," since "multiculturalism implies that some cultures may not be included, while diversity equalizes categories." This seems promising, since such a move seems to avoid the distinction between "majority" and "minority" cultures. Indeed, Steinberg goes on to say, the reality is that all such categories "eventually need to be dropped," and that doing so "would require the total re-working of all existing curricula and the absence of dominant cultural curricula as the bar with which *everything else* is measured." We seem to be inching closer to Fanon's "agenda for total disorder" that is decolonization.

But then Steinberg steps back from the edge, and in doing so, shows us the limitations of trying to work within the accepted understandings of these terms and the harsh limitations imposed by our current institutions: "I don't think we are quite ready for this. So . . . small steps. And with these small steps, we create equity."[11] Europe gets to remain on its platform, but a few folding

11   Shirley R. Steinberg, ed. *Diversity and Multiculturalism: A Reader* (New York: Peter Lang, 2009), p. xii-xiii.

chairs will be set up around it, in the name of diversity; order has been restored.

For our purposes, then, quibbling over the distinction between these two terms or the reasons for preferring one over the other won't get us very far. So I will suggest something simpler, by way of a three-part proposition:

1) The contemporary university is what we're left with when institutions—using subtle ideological coercion but also brute force—reconfigure radical student demands seeking to transform the system into convenient slogans that can help strengthen their brand.

2) In this context, **diversity** is what becomes of radical struggles around anti-racism when the demands of student and youth movements—movements that aimed (and continue to aim) not simply to "diversify" but to desegregate and ultimately decolonize the university—are torn from their basis in grassroots political movements.

3) In this same context, **multiculturalism** is what becomes of the radical internationalism at the heart of these student and youth movements when institutions substitute *cultural tolerance* for *political solidarity.*

When institutions even bother to try to distinguish between these terms, this is the general idea: *diversity* describes the management of what we might call "domestic" forms of difference (i.e. racial difference), while *multiculturalism* is about the management of difference on an international scale—although administrators prefer to use the word "global," which doesn't have all the dangerously radical resonances of "internationalism."

What we must remember is that for the radical student and youth movements whose repression gave rise to the neoliberal university, anti-racism and internationalism were (and are) inseparable. So decolonizing multiculturalism involves reviving that conjunction and orienting ourselves around *an anti-racist (and, not incidentally, anti-capitalist) internationalism.* Far from splitting hairs about the distinctions between "diversity" and "multiculturalism," our work is to completely refuse this distinction as it currently exists.

The Dream of a Black University: Diversification as Transformation

Let's stay with this question of diversity and anti-racism. If you track the relationship between them, and the ways that the term "diversity" has been variously used, you'll find a tension that remains today.[12] On the one hand, an emphasis on diversity was a major aspect of the US Civil Rights Movement from its inception. In its etymological sense, the word had not traditionally carried a positive connotation, and as we've already seen, in a context where setting up an "American" monoculture was a key part of the settler colonial foundations of this country, diversity was not at all on the agenda. For a Civil Rights Movement whose initial task involved overturning Jim Crow laws and institutions set up under the legal principle of "separate but equal" in the early to mid-twentieth century, an important part of this work involved forging a new understanding of "diversity" as a positive value rather than a problem.

The Supreme Court's 1954 decision in *Brown v. Board of Education* marks the extent to which this struggle was able to achieve some hard-won successes, at least within certain circumscribed zones. The innovative argument made by Thurgood Marshall and other members of the NAACP's Legal Defense Fund in *Brown*

12 Much of what follows has been deeply influenced by Nick Mitchell's brief but brilliant overview of "diversity" as a keyword in African American studies; go read it if you haven't: Nick Mitchell, "Diversity," in *Keywords for African American Studies*, ed. Erica R. Edwards, Roderick A. Ferguson, and Jeffrey O. G. Ogbar (New York: New York University Press, 2018).

and similar cases involved directly challenging and ultimately refuting the "but" in the doctrine of "separate but equal." When *Brown* was being argued before the Supreme Court, Justice Felix Frankfurter asked Marshall to define what he meant by "equal"; Marshall's famous reply was: "Equal means getting the same thing, at the same time, and in the same place." The Court ultimately agreed, declaring: "Separate educational facilities are inherently unequal."

At the heart of the decision was the idea that segregation was itself a form of harm that disallowed any possibility of "equality" between segregated institutions. The harm of segregation was primarily visited upon Black students, of course, but the argument that separate educational facilities were inherently unequal also implied that segregation ultimately damaged the society as a whole. "Diversity" named the condition of equality as defined by Marshall: a diverse institution was one in which everyone, in spite of their differences (racial or otherwise), could get the same thing at the same time in the same place. Far from threatening those who benefitted from segregation, diversity was thereafter intended to be understood as a good to be enjoyed equally by all.

In the years that followed, the question of what "diversity" should signify was very much up for grabs, especially within the university. Universities throughout the United States began to desegregate, although getting institutions to carry out in practice what was enshrined in law never happened without widespread struggles and violent backlash. The iconography of desegregation comes almost exclusively from the Deep South and the early 1960s: images of federal troops sent into Alabama and Mississippi to protect Black students from white rioters, escorting students into newly desegregated schools past screaming white mobs. But resistance to desegregation was never just a southern thing. Take the City University of New York—seemingly the diametrical opposite of Ole Miss and Bama. It was still, in practice, a segregated university in 1969, fifteen years after *Brown v. Board of Education*. Like their counterparts in the south, students fighting to desegregate CUNY faced the full violence of the police and angry white mobs before achieving their hard-won successes.

The mobilization required to truly desegregate universities (on the ground rather than just on paper) came primarily from anti-racist student movements. These movements in turn demanded that the institutions that had finally, and reluctantly, agreed to admit them take the next step and begin to represent the realities and experiences of the communities from which they came. That meant, among other things, demands for fundamental changes to curricula and calls for new disciplines and departments that would break with the monocultural tradition that had passed for "American culture" for nearly two centuries.

Toni Cade Bambara's 1969 essay "Realizing the Dream of a Black University," inspired by student uprisings at City College, eloquently enshrines the possibilities of this moment. Bambara, best known for her work as a writer of short fiction and as a filmmaker, had a long and active relationship with CUNY: she was a student at Queens College and City College in the 1950s before helping to establish CUNY's "Search for Education, Elevation, Knowledge" (SEEK) program in 1965. The SEEK program was designed to recruit and prepare students from communities that had historically been excluded from the university. Bambara draws on her full range of knowledge and experience in "Realizing the Dream of a Black University," which lays bare the problem for public universities that were reluctantly acknowledging the demand to expand beyond their traditional (white, male, class privileged) constituencies without a concomitant willingness to expand and transform the work of the university accordingly:

> The drift toward mass education was just that—a
> drifting. It grew out of some sloppily defined egois-
> tic devotion to the myth of democracy. . . . No one
> knew when, how, why, or in what way the universi-
> ties would have to shift their focus to accommodate
> a mass studentry, how the traditional approaches and
> traditional material would prove invalid once the
> new students came in, or how the traditional prem-
> ises might be challenged when the doors opened and
> in flocked people who were not part of the aristo-
> cratic classes. . . . judging by the state of health of the
> existing curriculum, they played havoc with the tra-
> ditional education, but not enough for our purposes.

As she notes, the move towards truly public education began after World War II, with the admission of
working-class students through the G.I. Bill and other
New Deal initiatives. Black communities were largely
excluded from those earlier initiatives, but thanks to the
gains of the Civil Rights Movement in the 1960s, students from minoritized communities were finally being
admitted as well. These students, who had managed to
force their way through the university's gates, were now
in a position to make possible the transformations needed
to make public universities truly public at last. Bambara
is unsparing about what the nature of that work must be:
"fissures or breaks are not enough. To obtain a relevant,

real education, we shall have to either topple the university or set up our own."[13]

Bambara's essay was first published in *Observation Post*, a newspaper produced by City College students, in February 1969. Two months later, members of the Black and Puerto Rican student community took control of City College and white students allied with their struggle occupied Klapper Hall, which housed the college's School of Education. The student occupiers renamed Klapper Hall "Huey P. Newton Hall for Political Action" and City College itself was declared "Harlem University." Such student protesters rightly understood that the transformation of universities in the wake of the gains won by the Civil Rights Movement was in their hands. Part of the fight was for inclusion—for example, one demand was that the racial composition of all entering classes reflect the Black and Puerto Rican population of all New York City's high schools—but it was also

13   Toni Cade Bambara, "Realizing the Dream of a Black University," *Observation Post*, vol. 45, no. 3 (February 14, 1969). Bambara's essay has been republished as part of the invaluable "Lost and Found" series produced by the CUNY Poetics Document Initiative: see Toni Cade Bambara, *"Realizing the Dream of a Black University" & Other Writings*, edited by Makeba Lavan and Conor Tomás Reed (Lost and Found, Series 7, Number 2, Fall 2017).

for the right to control their destiny at their institution and to help determine the content of their education. Student protesters demanded the creation of a School of Black and Puerto Rican Studies and that all education majors be required to study Black and Puerto Rican History and the Spanish language. And they made these demands both from within their own communities but also in solidarity with international struggles, against "a society that spills our blood needlessly in wars against the colored peoples of the world."[14]

What Bambara described and CUNY students enacted in 1969 was part of a widespread set of interconnected movements. Student movements demanded the establishment of programs that aimed to challenge and ultimately overthrow the monocultural "American" tradition. Demands were set out for programs in Black studies, ethnic studies, women's studies, third world studies. A diverse university, for these movements, meant a transformed university—not simply one that let in a few "diverse" students and then went on with business as usual, but one based on a very different understanding

14   Quotes are taken from a communique written by student protesters that has come to be called the "Newton Hall Statement"; it can be found as part of the online *CUNY Digital History Project*, an invaluable participatory archive of documents and interviews.

of who "belonged" in a university, what the purpose of a university should be, and indeed what knowledge production itself should look like. In doing so, these student movements linked local struggles to international ones, supporting and drawing inspiration from global struggles for decolonization. To follow the logic of these movements to its conclusion: in order to live up to the potential that anti-racist movements had invested in the word "diversity," a truly diverse university needed to be a decolonized university.

Lewis Powell's Counterrevolution

The managers of these universities had a very different idea of what "diversity" should mean, of course. I'm using the word "managers" rather than "administrators" here intentionally. Part of the counterinsurgency launched against student-led demands to decolonize the university, as we saw in the previous chapter, involved direct, deadly state violence aimed at student protesters. But another part of this counterinsurgency involved turning "diversity" from a word describing the aspiration towards revolutionary change to an administrative category used to manage difference and maintain the status quo. That effort involved university administrators, but also elected officials, corporations, legal institutions including the Supreme Court, and the police. The relative success of this managerial counterinsurgency has created diversity's current institutional life, painfully summarized by Nick Mitchell: "Diversity . . . is about difference but also about its overcoming—the promise that difference, properly conditioned, either will make *no difference* or, better yet, will transform difference into an asset primed for accumulation."[15]

For public universities, this counterattack on the aspirations of student movements has been accomplished in part via simple economics. At City College and throughout CUNY, what followed desegregation was not transformation but immiseration. Economic austerity programs pegged to white flight from the city decimated public services and led to huge cuts for public education, from primary schools to public universities. That had a direct effect upon the dreams of a Black university that had begun to emerge in the 1960s. Following the numbers tells the sad story of a decade: the number of Black and Puerto Rican students attending CUNY increased by more than 170 percent between 1969 and 1972, but beginning in 1975, following massive budget cuts, CUNY began charging tuition, and by 1980, the

15   Mitchell, "Diversity," p. 69, emphasis in original.

number of Black and Latino students entering CUNY had declined by fifty percent. Segregation comes in many forms, and economic austerity has proven to be just as effective as racist white mobs or cops at the gates.

But the austerity imposed upon universities by the state and eagerly seized upon by its managers had a further effect. Some of the institutional changes demanded by students included the establishment of programs in Black studies, women's studies, ethnic studies, and other radical forms of knowledge production. Many such programs were set up, but in most cases, these programs were woefully underfunded and thus designed to make them intrinsically marginal to the "traditional" work of the university. For example, they were often set up as "programs" or "concentrations" or "centers" rather than departments or housed within existing departments, were rarely given sufficient funding or the ability to hire faculty or recruit students, and thus were kept in a perpetual state of precarity. This in turn limits their ability to challenge the institution that pays the bills (sort of) and enables them to keep doing their work. In short, these programs were never allowed to forget that they were marginal. The message, read out of the numbers rather than the rhetoric, is clear: we're happy to include you, but never forget that you don't really belong here.

One way of telling this history is via the unlikely figure of Lewis F. Powell, who resides at the heart of this counterrevolution like a gross spider at the center of a web. Powell's career spanned many of the sites that came into play against student movements to decolonize the university. At Washington and Lee University in his native Virginia, he studied both law and commerce, and was president of his segregated fraternity. After receiving a law degree from Harvard he served as an intelligence officer in the Army. His long career as a lawyer and political figure spanned both the public and private spheres: he served as Chairman of the Richmond School Board at a time when the state of Virginia was using all its means to resist desegregation (like most white school officials, Powell remained silent on the issue) while working as a partner in a prominent corporate law firm. In October 1971, he was appointed to the Supreme Court by President Nixon, and served until his retirement in 1987.

Powell's first direct contribution to the campus counterrevolution came a few months before his appointment to the Supreme Court, when he was commissioned by the U.S. Chamber of Commerce, a lobbying group for businesses across the country, to write a confidential memorandum. Titled "Attack on the

American Free Enterprise System" (though it has come to be known simply as "The Powell Memorandum"— sounds ominous, no?), the premise was simple and clear: "No thoughtful person can question that the American economic system is under broad attack."[16] Powell had been enlisted by the Chamber of Commerce to offer a strategy for a counterattack. He was well positioned to do so: during his decades working as a corporate lawyer, his clients included the Tobacco Institute, and Powell himself was a board member of the Philip Morris tobacco company, best known for spending millions of dollars to convince people that cigarettes were good for you. The memo he produced took aim not just at the usual suspects—"Communists, New Leftists, and other revolutionaries"—but also against New Deal policies and the work of reformers such as Ralph Nader, who he declared to be "perhaps the single most effective antagonist of American business."

16   Lewis Powell, "Attack on American Free Enterprise System,"
     August 23, 1971. Powell's memorandum is widely available
     online. For critical analyses of the Powell Memorandum and its
     effects, see David Harvey, *A Brief History of Neoliberalism* (New
     York: Oxford UP, 2007); Lawrence B. Glickman, "Business as
     Usual: The Long History of Corporate Personhood," *Boston
     Review* (August 23, 2017); and Roderick Ferguson, *We Demand:
     The University and Student Protests* (Berkeley: U of California
     P, 2017), p. 35-53.

The Powell Memorandum was part of an emerging political strategy by corporate America. For David Harvey, one of the key theorists of neoliberalism, the Powell Memorandum marks the beginning of a major political and economic shift. Powell's main argument was that the supposed anti-business climate in the US had gone too far, and that business leaders needed to fight back. Harvey describes the response that followed: "After that we see the formation of a whole set of think tanks [and] the massing of money by various organizations to try to influence public policy and to do it through the media."[17] As a result, our collective attitude towards corporations today is much warmer and fuzzier than it was fifty years ago.

Writing his memo in 1971, Powell saw the university as both a site from which some of the most important attacks on the system were emanating and also as a strategic location from which corporations could counterattack—once the ground had been properly prepared, of course. Much of his memo is essentially an instruction manual explaining how corporations could seize back control of the university from wild-eyed students and faculty who he claimed were carrying out

17   "On Neoliberalism: An Interview with David Harvey," *Monthly Review* (June 19, 2006).

a "broad, shotgun attack on the system itself." Powell scolds the free enterprise system for not just tolerating but participating in its own destruction; after all, he notes pointedly, "The campuses from which much of the criticism emanates are supported by (i) tax funds generated largely from American business, and (ii) contributions from capital funds controlled or generated by American business." While Powell doesn't state explicitly that corporations should grab the universities by the purse strings to compel them to get in line, that's what he implies, and that's more or less what came to happen.

The Powell Memorandum set out a number of strategies for taking back the university from those wooly radicals who supposedly had come to control it: creating PR campaigns to confront critiques of the free market; providing funding to create an academic cadre of pro-capitalist faculty; evaluating textbooks to ensure "fair and factual treatment of our system of government and our system of free enterprise" (Powell took particular exception to the efforts of civil rights and labor union activists to "rewrite" textbooks); funding business schools; monitoring the way the free market system was being covered by the media; and restoring "balance" to universities by insisting that they hire pro-capitalist faculty to counter influential radical intellectuals like

Herbert Marcuse (who was Angela Davis' academic mentor). This last plank in the strategy is particularly important for the development of institutional "diversity" as we have come to know it today, since Powell makes his appeal for the "inclusion" of pro-capitalist voices on campus *in the name of diversity*. His legacy lives on today in the form of conservative appeals for "viewpoint diversity," which equate right-wing demands for equal time with efforts to redress the historical exclusion of minoritized communities.

Powell's memo thus provided a blueprint for a right-wing intellectual movement that has effectively taken control of the academic world that it once railed against. It was a first step in Powell's later effort, as a member of the Supreme Court, to establish the principle of "corporate personhood": that is, the idea that legally speaking, "corporations were literally understood as life-forms whose rights must be defended against the challenges put to them by actual people."[18] The Supreme Court's *Citizens United* decision of 2010 is the most famous, and most disastrous, result

18 Ferguson, *We Demand*, p. 41-43; see also Jeffrey Clements, "The Real History of 'Corporate Personhood': Meet the Man to Blame for Corporations Having More Rights Than You," *Alternet* (December 6, 2011).

of this philosophy. Beyond that, the strategies laid out in the Powell Memorandum led to the formation of powerful right-wing think tanks like the American Enterprise Institute, the Heritage Foundation, and the Manhattan Institute, institutions that have had a massive influence on economic and political policies over the past fifty years—not to mention sending an endless stream of right-wing talking heads to swarm upon the public sphere, largely drowning out the voices of university-based intellectuals.

The Powell Memorandum also inspired a young up-and-comer named Charles Koch to lend his support to the "fight for free enterprise" on campus. As the work of the impressive activist group Un-Koch My Campus has uncovered, today more than 300 universities receive direct funding from the Charles Koch Foundation; the Koch-funded Association for Private Enterprise Education has become a pipeline for pro-business faculty who are hired not just at universities but at influential think tanks and educational nonprofits; and the Koch model of exercising direct influence in exchange for much-needed donations has had a measurable effect on academic freedom, from decisions regarding the hiring of faculty to curricular decisions to decisions to provide or withdraw funding from student organizations.

As Charles' little brother David Koch put it, saying the quiet part out loud: "If we're going to give a lot of money, we'll make darn sure they spend it in a way that goes along with our intent. And if they make a wrong turn and start doing things we don't agree with, we withdraw funding."[19]

Who Owns Diversity?

The student movements of the 1960s had issued a fundamental challenge to business as usual at their universities. Inspired by a vision of diversity that was central to the Civil Rights Movement, they demanded that the desegregation of the university lead to its transformation. A transformed university would be one with students at its center: "You will not shut your eyes any longer," a leader of the student movement at Brooklyn College declared to the university's leaders. "Brooklyn College belongs to us, not you."[20] With Lewis Powell's memo in hand, the

19 Two important reports produced by "Un-Koch My Campus" are *Exposing the Association of Private Enterprise Education (APEE): Charles Koch's Network of Weaponized Professors* (2018) and *Violations of Academic Freedom, Faculty Governance, and Academic Integrity: An Analysis of the Charles Koch Foundation* (2018); both are available online.

20 Martha Biondi, "'Brooklyn College Belongs to Us': Black Students and the Transformation of Public Higher Education in

corporate world offered its response: actually, it belongs to us, and we'll be taking it back. Insofar as diversity would be allowed to exist, it would need to adapt to business as usual.

Two months after writing "Attack on the American Free Enterprise System," Powell was nominated to the Supreme Court by President Nixon. It was from there that he made his second important contribution to the evolution of today's neoliberal university. Powell wrote the Court's decision in the 1978 case *Bakke v. Regents of the University of California*, a ruling that was crucial in enshrining the current institutional model of "diversity." The case was one of several challenges to university-based affirmative action programs in the mid-1970s; it centered on a program established by the medical school at the University of California at Davis, which set aside a certain number of seats for applicants from what were defined as "disadvantaged backgrounds," primarily to address deep racial inequalities in medical school admissions. Allen Bakke, a thirty-five-year-old white man who had twice been rejected by the program, sued the university, claiming that he had been denied admission on the basis of his race.

New York City," in Clarence Thomas, ed., *Civil Rights in New York City* (New York: Fordham University Press, 2011), p. 166.

The case eventually made its way to the Supreme Court, which responded with a deeply divided opinion. Four justices argued that the university's affirmative action program was an illegal "quota system" and should be struck down; another four justices (including Thurgood Marshall, who had been appointed to the Supreme Court in 1967) argued that the program, like other affirmative action initiatives that aimed to remedy the history of racial disenfranchisement and exclusion, was Constitutional and should be allowed to continue. Justice Powell provided a bridge between the two sides. On the one hand, he agreed with the conservative justices that UC Davis' system was an unconstitutional quota system, since it used race as its sole factor; the Court thus ruled that the program should be struck down and Bakke should be admitted to the school. However, Powell also agreed with the liberal justices that race *could* be used in making affirmative action decisions, provided it was not the *only* criteria used to judge candidates. As a result, the Court's decision did not set aside all affirmative action programs, and thus was generally seen at the time as a vindication of the larger impetus towards affirmative action in college admissions.

Some legal scholars have described Powell's balancing act in forming an uneasy consensus for the Court's ruling as "Solomonic," while others have found the basis of his argument to be "deeply flawed."[21] In any case, the most lasting aspect of Powell's decision is that he made his argument that race could be used as a criterion among others in university admissions by appealing to the importance of *diversity*. In fact, Powell dismissed all other rationales presented for UC Davis' affirmative action program, including the need to redress the historical injustices of racial disenfranchisement or the ongoing inequality in educational opportunities, which he claimed was an inadequate reason to support such programs—thus undermining the main political argument for affirmative action as a form of anti-racism. The *only* compelling rationale for upholding certain affirmative action programs that used race as a criteria, according to Powell, was the argument that *the university itself stood to benefit from diversity*. As he wrote in his decision, "the goal of achieving a diverse student body is sufficiently compelling to justify consideration of race in admissions decisions under some circumstances."[22]

21   Anthony Lewis, "A Solomonic Decision," *The New York Times* (June 29, 1978); Randall Kennedy, *For Discrimination: Race, Affirmative Action, and the Law* (New York: Pantheon, 2013), p. 199.

22   *Bakke v. Regents of the University of California*, quoted in Mitchell, "Diversity," p. 71-72.

In other words, "diversity" was no longer part of the effort to address and redress the long history of discrimination and oppression and to avoid their continuation in the present, as it had been for the Civil Rights Movement and for student movements aiming to desegregate and decolonize their universities. Rather, it was now to be understood simply as an attractive outcome whose benefits would be reaped by institutions, whether universities or corporations, and only indirectly (if at all) by those minoritized communities who actually constituted this "diversity."

There's an important link between Powell's 1971 memorandum and his decision in *Bakke v. Regents* seven years later. In the intermingling of these two texts lies the basis for the institutionalization of "diversity" as difference management. When university administrators declare that they "value multicultural diversity," they are certainly expressing their rhetorical commitment to diversity as a valuable—in the sense of generally good—thing. But embedded in that statement is the fact that diversity is literally *economically valuable*—"an asset primed for accumulation"—and that the university itself gets to be the recipient of that value.

Angela Davis was already tracking this institutionalization of diversity at the time Powell was writing his

Bakke decision. In an essay published a few years later, she noted the extent to which corporate models of "diversity management" were beginning to dominate universities: the goal of such strategies was to manage diversity so that ultimately "difference doesn't make any difference, if only we acquire knowledge about it." She uses the example of an article written by a corporate strategist entitled "Get Ready to Manage a Salad Bowl." The message of such diversity management approaches was "that a racially, ethnically, and culturally heterogeneous workforce needs to be managed or controlled in ways that contain and suppress conflict."[23] The inevitable result is that diversity becomes, not the culmination of the demands for decolonization made by anti-racist movements but instead an asset that, properly acquired and managed, is consumed by institutions. "A salad consisting of many ingredients," Davis notes pointedly, "is colorful and beautiful, and it is to be consumed by someone." That distinguishes terms like "difference" and "diversity" from the term "racism," which "sharply calls for redress of historical and current grievances." That's why, Davis concludes, "I get more excited at a

23 Angela Davis, "Gender, Class, and Multiculturalism: Rethinking 'Race' Politics," in Gordon and Newfield, *Mapping Multiculturalism*, p. 46.

Public Enemy concert when I hear young people chanting 'Fuck racism' (even though I might find problematic
moments in the performance) than in a discussion on
'recognizing diversity.'"[24]

The managers of the neoliberal university are
unlikely to join in that chorus of "Fuck racism," since
they aren't particularly keen on redressing historical and
current grievances. It's so much easier to position diversity as a good and promising thing that is ultimately to
everyone's benefit, but which nevertheless needs to be
carefully managed to avoid "conflict." This approach,
which Davis refers to as "the disciplining of diversity,"
is clearly visible today when administrators respond to
political challenges by demanding "civility" from the
university's students and workers alike.

I was reminded of this when I and other faculty
at my college tried to open a public discussion about
the revelation that an adjunct professor who had taught
psychology at Kingsborough for at least five years
was, under a different name, also a prominent white
supremacist who co-hosted a podcast with the odious
neo-Nazi Richard Spencer. We objected to the fact that
the college administration's response to this horrifying

24   Davis, "Gender, Class, and Multiculturalism," p. 41, 44-45.

revelation had been radio silence—likely an attempt to avoid bad publicity and possible legal repercussions, the two things that administrators fear the most. In response to our attempt to foster further discussion of the situation, our college president publicly chided us for being "unprofessional" and "not collegial." No further discussion ensued. In this manner, diversity was very effectively managed.[25]

"A Euphemism for a Plainer Word That Has Apparently Become Unspeakable"

If the goodness that resides in diversity comes from its value—economic and otherwise—to institutions, including corporation-persons, then the term itself can be put to a variety of contradictory uses. Jonathan Kozol, who has documented the extent to which K-12 education in the US has been systematically *re*-segregated over the past several decades, creating what he calls an "apartheid education" system, notes that the term *diversity*—once a major tool in the struggle for desegregation—has been put to work in the service of

25   For the full story, see Jake Offenhartz, "NYC Psychology Professor Secretly Moonlights as White Nationalist Co-Host of Richard Spencer's Podcast," *Gothamist* (November 8, 2019) and Anthony Alessandrini, "TFW Your Former Colleague Turns Out to Be a Nazi," *Academe Blog* (December 9, 2019).

this process of re-segregation, with sometimes mind-boggling results. Kozol describes a visit to a school in St. Louis, Missouri, where he is given a handout describing how the school's curriculum "addresses the needs of children from diverse backgrounds." When he is provided with the school's demographic statistics, however, he discovers that 99.6 percent of students there were African American. Another school in New York that referred proudly to "the diversity" of its student population and "the rich variations of ethnic backgrounds" had numbers that directly belied this claim: there were 2,800 Black and Hispanic students, 1 Asian child, and 3 whites. "Visitors to schools like these," Kozol concludes, "discover quickly the eviscerated meaning of the word [diversity], which is no longer a proper adjective but a euphemism for a plainer word [segregation] that has apparently become unspeakable."[26] So goes the story, fifty years after *Brown v. Board of Education*: segregated schools serving students from minoritized communities are declared to be "diverse";

26 Jonathan Kozol, "Still Separate, Still Unequal: America's Educational Apartheid," *Harper's* (September 2005). For an extended account, see Kozol's book *The Shame of the Nation: The Restoration of Apartheid Schooling in America* (New York: Random House, 2005).

segregated schools serving white students declare that they value "diversity."

But institutions can play this substitution game in the other direction as well. In 2014, the data firm Priceonomics put out a report that claimed to list "The Most and Least Diverse Cities in America." The city that topped the list of *least diverse* cities was Detroit, with a population of 80.7 percent African American residents (just ahead of El Paso, with a 79.7 percent Hispanic/ Latino population). Here the same sorts of demographics used by school districts to describe themselves as "diverse" (and *definitely not segregated*) are deployed in the exact opposite manner: a numerical majority of African American residents is used "as evidence of Black *dominance*, a dominance presented as a problem that diversification can solve," as Nick Mitchell writes. And not without reason, since from this entrepreneurial vantage point, the "solution" to the problem of Detroit needs to come via the sort of (economic) "diversification" that could only be provided by (white) gentrification.[27]

To sum up: in one of these instances, *diversity* comes to function as a substitute for the word "apartheid"; in the other, it "provides a progressive patina to the political and economic forces driving the displacement of

27   Mitchell, "Diversity," p. 74.

poor and working-class black Detroiters."[28] Now that the term has been effectively severed from struggles for social justice and redistribution, it all just depends on what capital needs the word to mean at any particular time and place.

So *decolonizing diversity* must be part of our agenda for total disorder. As with *multiculturalism*, historicizing the term offers us an opportunity to unleash its potential as a critical tool that might be taken up for decolonization, rather than dominance. Reclaiming the radical legacy embodied in the term as it was used by anti-racist movements enables us to embrace the potential critical value of *diversity* by "emphasizing its usefulness as a lens for training attention on racial capitalism in its material and ideological transits."[29]

That's exactly what contemporary student and youth movements have done. Since the primary focus of this chapter has been on the counterrevolution against the student movements of the 1960s, it seems important to end with the reminder that the work initiated by those movements, while it has come under constant attack, has never been abandoned. For Lewis Powell and his followers, the university was the site from which

28   Mitchell, "Diversity," p. 74.

29   Mitchell, "Diversity," p. 68.

to launch a counterattack against those fighting for a transformed society, but it remains a site of ongoing struggle. That becomes clear in the Policy Platform produced by the Movement for Black Lives. In a section outlining the demand for reparations, the first demand involves access to universities—not as part of a strategy of mere "inclusion" but rather with an eye towards reparative transformation:

> [We demand] reparations for the systemic denial of access to high quality educational opportunities in the form of full and free access for all Black people (including undocumented and currently and formerly incarcerated people) to lifetime education including: free access and open admissions to public community colleges and universities, technical education (technology, trade and agricultural), educational support programs, retroactive forgiveness of student loans, and support for lifetime learning programs.

The Movement for Black Lives' demands for educational reparations echoes both the content and also the larger spirit of the Five Demands issued by the student groups that occupied City College in 1969, which have now become an honored part of the history of student movements. Five decades later, as the COVID-19 pandemic decimated New York, the Free CUNY coalition drew on this oppositional history in setting out their own version of the Five Demands, demanding, among other things, a tax on the massive wealth that had been redistributed upwards in the years since Powell exhorted the business world to fight back.[30]

The counterrevolutionary forces of "order" have many weapons at their disposal. Some are metaphorical; some fire real bullets. But the dream of a decolonized university lives on.

30 See the online petition "Five Demands to Heal CUNY in Crisis," first launched in May 2020.

Chapter Six

KEEP THE STUDENTS OUT OF THE BOARDROOM, OR THE UNIVERSITY MUST BE PROTECTED!

Let's return to Nixon's Commission on Campus Unrest, established after the state murders at Kent State and Jackson State in 1970. As we've seen, the Commission's report used the occasion of deadly state violence against student protesters to portray these protesters as themselves responsible for violence and disorder—in short, as criminals. The militarized campus built in the aftermath of this report takes this logic to its conclusion: since any student could potentially be a protester, it follows that any student is potentially a criminal. More specifically, the Commission's report accuses student protesters of creating *disorder*, which it defines as part of a continuum that begins with "disruption," extends to "violence," and ends in "terrorism." By collapsing this continuum into the word "disorder," the report provides a powerful rhetorical weapon that can be wielded against student protesters. After all, according to this logic, the "disorder" created by any disruption of the university's work—including nonviolent actions like sit-ins, strikes, or the occupation of a building—becomes equated with the threat of violent terrorism.

This logic, by which students are criminalized based on their potential to create "disorder," continues to govern campus policing. But the Commission's report also offers a slight mitigation of this criminality, since student protesters are also said to be acting *irrationally.* What we have here, in other words, is simply a failure to communicate—or rather, a situation marked by what the Commission's experts on unrest describe as "a crisis of understanding." Students have some legitimate complaints, the report acknowledges, but the protesters just go too far. They refuse to recognize the importance of balance, of hearing both sides of things. They show an "impatience" with the slow grinding procedures of liberal democracy and "a growing denial of the humanity and good will of those who urge patience and restraint, and particularly of those whose duty is to enforce the law." And, most important, student protesters fail to recognize "that they are citizens of a nation which was founded on tolerance and diversity, and they must become more understanding of those with whom they differ."[1]

1   *Report of the President's Commission on Campus Unrest*, p. 4-6, 14, 131, quoted in Roderick A. Ferguson, *We Demand: The University and Student Protests* (Berkeley: U of California P, 2017), p. 22-23, 28-29.

In a funny sort of way, the Commission on Campus Unrest thus acknowledges the power and potential unleashed by the student protesters of their day. Just as Lewis Powell was not wrong to recognize the extent to which student movements were calling into question the dehumanizing power of capitalism, the Commission correctly notes that these movements were also questioning the fundamental bases on which their education—which is to say, their society—was built. This impulse is the first step on the road to decolonization.

But if students were intent on revealing the extent to which the United States was built upon a history of exploitation, racism, and colonization, defenders of the system such as Powell and Nixon's Commission would insist that the United States was a nation founded on "tolerance and diversity." By doing so—backed by the coercive power to make their narrative stick—they thus violently wrenched these terms away from those who were fighting for *actual* tolerance and diversity. Instead, a new equation was offered. If the university, that great representative of the nation's foundational ideas, was to be understood as the epicenter of tolerance and diversity, then by this logic student protesters attempting to disrupt the work of the university must be understood as *intolerant bigots*: enemies of diversity bent on destroying this bastion of tolerance.

Let the (White) Man Speak! The Tolerant Suppression of Disruption

Let's stay with this link made by the Commission's report between "disruption," violence, and the work of the university. *Disruption* is defined in the report as "any interference with others to conduct their rightful business." Examples of such "disruption" are said to include "sit-ins, interference with academic activities, the blockading of campus recruiters" (the Commission likely had military recruiters in mind), and "interference with the rights of others to speak or to hear others speak."[2] You might notice that all these forms of "disruption" are tactics used by the Civil Rights Movement and other movements engaged in nonviolent civil disobedience. You might also realize that this incredibly broad definition of "disruption" means that literally any attempt to interrupt business as usual on campus is, from the standpoint of the administration and the campus police, on the same continuum as an act of violent terrorism.

This might sound like an exaggeration. But think about it from the perspective of the administrator-cop: if the university claims to be the great guardian of tolerance and diversity, then it must protect these values

2   *Report of the President's Commission on Campus Unrest*, p. 117, quoted in Ferguson, *We Demand*, p. 28.

against any who threaten them; and if the business of the university is to spread tolerance and diversity, then any interruption of this business can only be understood as intolerance and anti-diversity. It might seem that students protesting on campus are attempting to exercise their civil liberties. Wrong, says the administration: by interfering with the business of the university, students themselves are the ones stifling free expression. Thus, this broad definition of *disruption* has the result of "justifying police repression in the name of order and relying on the university administration—and not the faculty or students—to determine what is the rightful business of the university and what is not, what is orderly and what is not."[3]

In short, the forces of tolerance and diversity will brook neither dissent nor disruption.

This violent defense of "tolerance" by administrators, backed up by the campus police, ultimately empowers racist voices while suppressing anti-racist student movements attempting to take back their campuses from right-wing "experts" whose views make a mockery of the idea of "tolerance." When the noted racist Charles Murray—author of *The Bell Curve*, which makes a literal case for biological racial superiority and

3   Ferguson, *We Demand*, p. 29.

inferiority—was invited to speak at Middlebury College at the invitation of the college's American Enterprise Institute Club (Lewis Powell would fucking love that), student protesters disrupted the event by turning their backs on Murray as he began to speak and chanting "Your message is hatred, we will not tolerate it." The incident gained nationwide recognition when a small group of protesters subsequently confronted Murray and the professor who was moderating the event as they attempted to leave, allegedly causing injury to the professor.

Condemnations were swift and harsh. In the immediate aftermath, Laurie Patton, Middlebury's president, criticized the protesters, blaming them for "the lost opportunity for those in our community who wanted to listen to and engage with Mr. Murray." This of course ignores the fact that, as a famous intellectual who works at an influential think tank, Mr. Murray hardly lacks for platforms. President Patton eventually published an article in the *Wall Street Journal* with the condescending title "The Right Way to Protect Speech on Campus"—clearly, the students' attempt to oppose racism was the *wrong* way.[4]

4   Laurie Patton, "The Right Way to Protect Free Speech on Campus," *Wall Street Journal* (June 10, 2017).

Patton and others who criticized student protesters were keen to establish the difference between "legitimate" and "illegitimate" forms of campus protest: it all comes back to the question of *disruption*. "To be clear, I want to state that peaceful, non-disruptive protest is not only allowed at Middlebury, it is encouraged," the president wrote, making it clear that "disruptive" protest was thus not only discouraged, but forbidden. Soon after the Murray event, a group of Middlebury faculty issued a statement entitled "Free Inquiry on Campus"—published, once again, in the *Wall Street Journal*—that denounced the student protesters and declared a set of "principles" that would supposedly guarantee academic freedom. Again, the line was drawn around "disruption": by declaring that "Students have the right to challenge and to protest non-disruptively the views of their professors and guest speakers," the professors' statement made it clear that disruption itself was a bridge too far.[5]

"Free Inquiry on Campus" claims to be an "unassailable" defense of academic freedom. But legal scholar Adam Sitze notes that this "peculiar" document fails to make any judgements about what forms of speech should or should not be allowed to circulate as "knowledge."

5   Jay Parini and Keegan Callanan et al., "Middlebury's Statement of Principle," *Wall Street Journal* (March 6, 2017).

Nor does it address the crucial question of a university's responsibility to establish the truth or falsity of important claims—even though it was written just months after the election of Donald Trump and the rise of Trumpian claims about "fake news."[6]

By contrast, Middlebury student protesters, who published their own response a few days later, addressed these questions directly. After all, they noted, Murray should be given credit for honesty: describing *The Bell Curve* to a *New York Times* reporter in 1994, he was clear that his goal was to make racism intellectually respectable: "A huge number of well-meaning whites fear that they are closet racists, and this book tells them they are not. It's going to make them feel better about things they already think but do not know how to say."[7] By opposing the standard liberal claim that openly racist figures deserve a platform on campus or that hateful views needed to be "respectfully engaged," the student protesters provide an eloquent vision for how a university might uphold academic freedom against the Murrays and Trumps of the world:

6   Adam Sitze, "Academic Unfreedom, Unacademic Freedom," *The Massachusetts Review* 58.4 (2017).

7   Jason Deparle, "Daring Research or 'Social Science Pornography'?: Charles Murray," *The New York Times Magazine* (October 9, 1994).

> By elevating bigotry and engaging with it in open debate under the misguided view that all ideas must be respected, we risk elevating biased opinions with no solid, factual foundation into the realm of "knowledge" and affirming the unconscious biases many hold. . . . If we hold that the contest of clashing viewpoints is the only way to solidify knowledge, it naturally follows that we have a responsibility to articulate some parameters for which viewpoints are worthy of such a process.[8]

These supposedly "intolerant" student protesters were in fact the only ones at Middlebury willing to engage with the difficult question of how to defend spaces of (relative) tolerance from the onslaught of intolerance. It was only the students who "at least tried to assume the responsibility of asking what constitutes specifically academic speech."[9] Those who attacked them, meanwhile, could do no better than to appeal to the standard logic of academic freedom at neoliberal universities: the defense of a "free marketplace of ideas." The "tolerance" here is the tolerance of the market: whatever sells, wins. The "openness" is that of the market: open for business! No wonder the views of the Middlebury administration and

8   "Broken Inquiry on Campus: A Response by a Collection of Middlebury Students" (March 12, 2017), quoted in Sitze, "Academic Unfreedom, Unacademic Freedom," p. 768-69.

9   Sitze, "Academic Unfreedom, Unacademic Freedom," p. 770.

their faculty supporters were published in the *Wall Street Journal*: what defenders of the status quo like best about the "marketplace of ideas" has less to do with ideas and more to do with the fact that it is a literal marketplace.

As a model for the university in the age of Trump, this is feeble stuff; as a response to the work of Charles Murray, an influential figure characterized by the Southern Poverty Law Center as a "white nationalist," it's completely unacceptable. But as long as students can be prevented from "disrupting" the university's business as usual, defenders of the system can continue to smugly claim that their principles are "unassailable."

It's a Riot! or, Call the Police, the Students Are Here

My firsthand experience of the inevitably violent results that come from defining students as a "disruptive" force came during a series of student protests at CUNY in November 2011.[10] CUNY's Board of Trustees was holding a meeting at Baruch College to discuss a proposed tuition increase (one of many such increases—tuition and fees have gone up more than 30 percent at CUNY since 2010). A protest had been going on outside for a

10   I wrote about this in detail at the time; see "Our University: On Police Violence at CUNY," *Jadaliyya* (November 27, 2011).

few hours when some of us began to enter the building in order to attend the BOT meeting—which was, like all such meetings, ostensibly open to the public. All of us entered the building holding our CUNY ID cards in hand. Most were CUNY students; a lot of them had signed up in advance to testify at the meeting, as instructed. A handful of us faculty and staff supporters were present to provide support.

Despite the obvious fact that a lot of people would want to attend a public meeting where a large tuition raise was being discussed, the Board were meeting in a small conference room on the fourteenth floor. As we entered the lobby, we found ourselves facing a phalanx of campus police with their truncheons drawn, positioned in a line between us and the turnstiles leading to the elevators. We would later learn that along with campus police from several CUNY campuses, members of the New York City Police Department were also stationed in the building. The CUNY administration initially denied this; however, their presence at Baruch violated a policy forbidding the NYPD to come on campus in non-emergency situations unless they were directly invited by the administration—which, in this case, they clearly were.

What happened next proceeded differently for different people in our group. For me, it involved being

violently and without warning shoved by campus security, using their batons, towards the exit; being told that
if I did not leave the lobby immediately, I would be
arrested; receiving no explanation when I asked (well,
under the circumstances, shouted repeatedly) what the
grounds would be for arresting an ID-holding member
of the CUNY faculty simply for being in the lobby of
a CUNY building where a public hearing was being
held, until one cop blurted out, "Because it's a riot!";
and, finally, being forcefully shoved out of the lobby via
a glass revolving door, the only remaining way out of
the building, since the violent response of the police had
succeeded in blocking the main exit.

For several students, things were much worse.
They were forced facedown onto the ground, pinned by
several officers, tightly handcuffed, and charged, surre-
ally, with "trespassing" in a building at their own university. At least a dozen students were handcuffed and
detained; five were subsequently placed under arrest
and brought to an NYPD precinct, where they were
held for hours (in some cases, overnight). Students who
had done nothing more than enter a university building were charged variously with criminal trespassing,
resisting arrest, and disorderly conduct. In one case, a
student who attempted to grab the truncheon that an
officer was using to smash him in the ribs received the

incredible charge of grand larceny. But for most of the students who were detained, the police stuck with a tried-and-true charge: "disorderly conduct."

Compared to the police violence unleashed against student protesters at other campuses that fall, when the Occupy movement was on the rise, that incident at CUNY was, sadly, relatively mild. Only a few days before, students at the University of California at Davis, who were also accused of "trespassing" on their own campus while protesting tuition increases, were systematically attacked with pepper spray by university police.[11] At Berkeley that same week, student protesters were viciously beaten by police officers, as were their faculty supporters. When Celeste Langan, a noted Wordsworth scholar, attempted to intervene to protect students, police dragged her away by her hair. Robert Hass, the seventy-year-old former Poet Laureate of the United States, was struck in the ribs with a truncheon; another poet, Geoffrey O'Brien,

11   Reynoso Task Force, *UC Davis November 18, 2011 "Pepper Spray Incident" Task Force Report* (March 2012). Five years later, the UC Davis administration spent $175,000 to consultants to "scrub the internet" of references to or photos of the pepper spray incident; in a bit of cosmic justice, news of the attempted cover-up then went viral. See Sarah Parvini, "UC Davis Spends $175,000 to Sanitize Its Online Image After Ugly Pepper Spray Incident," *Los Angeles Times* (April 14, 2016).

had his ribs broken by a police beating. Students returned to protest the next night carrying signs saying: "Beat Poets, not beat poets."[12]

Such incidents reveal the extent to which university administrators and the campus police see themselves as the protectors of order—that is to say, as guardians of the business of the university, which is also somehow the business of tolerance and diversity. If need be, students who interfere with that business will be savagely attacked in the name of tolerance and diversity. CUNY's initial statement about the police riot included the false claim that student protesters "surged forward toward the college's identification turnstiles, where they were met by CUNY Public Safety officers and Baruch College officials" (no mention of the NYPD officers who were also present). The administration also claimed that the "disturbance" in the lobby threatened to interrupt classes that were in session in the building. After a wealth of video evidence proved that none of this was true, the statement was quietly removed from the CUNY website.

In fact, what happened that afternoon was precisely the opposite: the police attacked the students not for surging forward but for sitting down—more specifically,

12 Robert Hass, "Poet-Bashing Police," *The New York Times* (November 19, 2011).

for taking part in a sit-in, an action made famous by the Civil Rights Movement. Prevented from entering a public meeting where they had hoped to provide testimony about an issue that would directly affect their education and their lives, student protesters opted instead to attempt to hold their own hearing in the lobby of the building. In a sense, they were simply re-occupying what was ostensibly their own university in order to conduct intellectual business of their own. It was at this point that the police themselves surged forward. "CUNY public safety officers and Baruch College officials" (not to mention our guests from the NYPD) were conducting the work of the university; it was not to be disrupted by students, or for that matter by professors.

"Things to Give Student-Activists that Exclude Their Original Demands"

To sum up: what student protesters are said to lack, and what those who propose to run the university claim to possess, is both *tolerance* and *respect for diversity.* Anyone who has spent a minute on a college campus will recognize these as the two keywords of institutional multiculturalism. The anti-racist, anti-capitalist, feminist, and anti-imperialist student and youth movements of the 1960s and 1970s, who demanded that the university become more democratic, more racially diverse, and more open, set in motion the energies that necessitated the development of institutional multiculturalism. But these energies were ultimately redirected and coopted by the state, corporations, and university administrators as part of the counterinsurgency carried out against these student movements. When the dust cleared, campuses were more firmly in the hands of university administrators than ever before. After all, if students were the agents of disruption, then it was up to administrators to be the guardians of tolerance and diversity—as these qualities had come to be institutionally understood. As long as the administrators were allowed to run things without disruption, there would be no need to call in the police, who remained the last line of defense standing between the tolerant, multicultural university and its unruly, disruptive students.

The basis for today's administrative university was clearly set out by Nixon's Commission on Campus Unrest back in 1970. Administrators were tasked with being the representatives of institutions which, like the nation itself, were said to be "founded on tolerance and diversity." Students simply needed to acknowledge "the humanity and good will" of administrators "who urge patience and restraint" and of the police "whose duty is to enforce the law." Most important, students needed to give up their intolerant views and "become more understanding of those with whom they differ."[13] When Charles Murray comes to speak, in other words, sit quietly and let Mr. Murray have his say, and if you are so moved, maybe you can write a scathing op-ed for the school newspaper the next day. That's how the *Wall Street Journal* would handle it!

It's obscene that Nixon's Commission on Campus Unrest, set up to address the murder of students on their own campuses by soldiers and police officers, would conclude that the whole problem stems from the failure of students to recognize the inherent "tolerance and diversity" of a system that could so blithely slaughter them in a hail of bullets. But the reader may recognize the evil refrain that's still part of the language used by this system of order to attack young people who dare to oppose it. The "intolerance" attributed to student protesters in the 1970s morphed into the threat of so-called "political correctness" beginning in the eighties and nineties. That phrase, and the culture warrior stance that it recalls, was very effectively revived by Trump in 2016.[14]

13   *Report of the President's Commission on Campus Unrest*, p. 4-6, 14, 131, quoted in Roderick A. Ferguson, *We Demand: The University and Student Protests* (Berkeley: U of California P, 2017), p. 22-23, 28-29.

14   "You watch him calculating, yet not seeming to care about the consequences of what he says, and you listen to his supporters enjoying the feel of his freedom. . . . [they] say, over and over:

Most recently, the same logic informs current attacks on the much-maligned, completely misunderstood, and mostly non-existent "cancel culture," a scourge that has exorcised and terrified some of the mightiest establishment intellectuals of our time.[15] Frothing commentators engage in "a curious intergenerational complaint: students these days are not only too soft (they are vulnerable snowflakes who melt in the heat of public dispute) but also too hard (they are incipient totalitarians whose overriding wish is to persecute dissenters)."[16] Idealizing the student protesters of the 1960s—safely dead and buried and thus unable to interrupt their rants—today's defenders of the system use this idealized image to attack "uncivil" student protesters who have the gall to try to keep white supremacists from being granted bully pulpits on their campuses.

If you've ever had the misfortune to sit through a meeting where university administrators meet with students to discuss their righteous political demands,

We're for Trump because he's not politically correct, PC has harmed America, and you think, *people feel so unfree.*" Lauren Berlant, "Trump, or Political Emotions," *The New Inquiry* (August 5, 2016).

15   See the now infamous "Letter on Justice and Open Debate," *Harper's Magazine* (July 7, 2020).

16   Sitze, "Academic Unfreedom, Unacademic Freedom," p. 589-90.

you'll immediately recognize how the logic set out by the Commission on Campus Unrest—students as intolerant and irrational, administrators as patient defenders of tolerance and diversity—continues to rule the day on campus. It's all on display: the oily show of sympathy for the students' "legitimate grievances" offered together with the "but surely you must understand . . . " excuses for not addressing them, quickly followed by the crushing infantilization of students' demands for real change via the insistence that they must be "practical" and not "irrational." Throughout it all, you'll note the constant repetition of the need for mutual respect, civility, patience, restraint—in short, the need to do things in an orderly manner. And if students still fail to understand the way that things work, then regrettably, the police will have to be called in.

Recall where Fanon asks us to begin: "Decolonization, which sets out to change the order of the world, is clearly an agenda for total disorder."[17]

In order to prevent the police from being called, which can lead to things becoming very disordered indeed, the Commission on Campus Unrest made an additional suggestion alongside the recommendation for

17 Frantz Fanon, *The Wretched of the Earth*, trans. Richard Philcox (New York: Grove, 2004), p. 2.

universities to set up armed campus police forces: a management strategy that the report calls "the ombudsman method." This involves appointing an administrative figure whose job is to "act as a mediator and factfinder for students, faculty members, and administrations." To perform this role, the ombudsman "must have both great autonomy and [the] support of the university president." These "special student affairs administrators" are described in a way that's unapologetically tokenistic. As an example of an ideal candidate, the report recommends "a young, independent, black [sic] administrator" who would "serve in the role of a spokesman, mediator, and advisor for black [sic] students. Because these administrators have the confidence of the students, they can suggest practical modifications of student demands without being automatically branded as 'sell-outs.'"[18]

Behold the invention of the diversity worker: autonomous and seemingly powerful, although they work at the pleasure of the president. The satirical job description of the Director of the Colorblind Rainbow Center for Campus Diversity, in the *McSweeney's* article I discussed in the previous chapter, includes as one of the job's most important responsibilities the duty of "developing

18   *Report of the President's Commission on Campus Unrest*, p. 205, quoted in Ferguson, *We Demand*, p. 24-25.

lists of things to give student-activists that exclude their original demands."[19] That's precisely how the "ombudsman method" was designed to work. It's the strategy that abolitionist scholar Dylan Rodriguez has recently described as "reformism as counterinsurgency."[20]

The unapologetic tokenism of such positions continues today as well. Upper-level university administrators (and, for that matter, tenured and tenure-track university faculty) remain overwhelmingly white and male—as of 2017, more than 58 percent of college presidents were white men. The one exception involves those lower-level administrators working in "student affairs," where day-to-day "diversity work" takes place. According to a 2019 report by the Association of American Colleges & Universities, "among offices on campus, student affairs was the most likely to have a person of color as its highest-level administrator." Overall, the report concludes, "Students were more likely to encounter people of color in service roles than in faculty or leadership

19   Tatiana McInnis and Amanda Lehr, "The Colorblind Rainbow Center for Campus Diversity Seeks a New Director to Tell Us That Nothing Is Wrong," *McSweeney's Internet Tendency* (July 8, 2020).

20   Dylan Rodriguez, "Reformism Isn't Liberation, It's Counterinsurgency," *Medium* (October 20, 2020).

positions. While people of color represented less than one-fifth of senior executives, 42.2 percent of service and maintenance staff and one-third of campus safety personnel were people of color."[21] There, in a nutshell, you'll find the balance of power in the contemporary multicultural university, which must be protected, at all costs, from the disruption of students.

I promised you a book that wasn't unrelievedly grim and negative. Let me therefore remind you that so far, I've only told half of the story.

Returning to the Roots

We've seen the extent to which today's university derives from that deft trick, in the wake of Kent State and Jackson State, of turning the state murder of students into an opportunity to increase managerial and police control. But it's important to emphasize that I follow the lead of other activist-scholars in seeing our contemporary "multicultural" university as emerging from the clash of two opposed forces. The effective neutralization of the most radical impulses of student movements by the state, corporations, and university administrations came via the violent smashing of

21   "College Students Are More Diverse Than Ever. Faculty and Administrators Are Not," *AAC&U News* (March 2019).

demands for decolonization, wrapped up in the pretty words offered by institutional multiculturalism. But the counterinsurgency of institutional multiculturalism would never have been necessary without the insurgent demands of student movements, particularly Black and Third-Worldist movements.[22] Remembering that history is the beginning of our work.

Faced with the grim reality of the university today, we need to remind ourselves of the significant and hard-won victories of student movements for decolonization. At San Francisco State, the country's first School of Ethnic Studies was established in 1969 following the longest student strike in US history. The struggle was led by a Third World Liberation Front that united the Black Student Union, Latin American Students Organization, Asian American Political Alliance, Filipino American Collegiate Endeavor, and Native American Students Union at SFSU—a radically multicultural alliance if there ever was one. Down the road a bit, at Berkeley, the Department of Ethnic Studies was created as a result of another student strike led by students united as the

22 I'm borrowing the notion of institutional multiculturalism as "counterinsurgency" from Jodi Melamed's *Represent and Destroy: Rationalizing Violence in the New Racial Capitalism* (Minneapolis: U of Minnesota P, 2011).

Third World Liberation Front. Less well known is the remarkable history of Merritt College, a two-year college in Oakland, where collaborations between students, faculty, and community activists resulted in the first Black history course in the country, initially offered in 1964, and the founding of the country's first Black Studies Department three years later. Huey P. Newton and Bobby Seale, the founders of the Black Panther Party, met while they were students there, and it's fair to say that Merritt College was the birthplace of the Panthers.[23]

At my own school, the City University of New York, the struggles of a united student movement led by Black and Puerto Rican student groups in the late 1960s and early 1970s succeeded not only in winning a program in Black and Puerto Rican Studies, but also a radical but sadly short-lived open enrollment policy. This student-led struggle to desegregate CUNY has been justly described as "the most significant civil rights victory in higher education in the history of

23 See Donna Jean Murch, *Living for the City: Migration, Education, and the Rise of the Black Panther Party in Oakland, California* (Chapel Hill: University of North Carolina Press, 2010), and the film *Merritt College: Home of the Black Panthers*, directed by Jeffrey Heyman and available online.

the United States."[24] And the struggle continues. The resounding "Five Demands" issued by students at City College in 1969 are echoed in the "Five Demands to Heal CUNY in Crisis" issued in 2020, at the height of the COVID-19 pandemic, by the Free CUNY Coalition.

This is the point where I'm supposed to say something vaguely apologetic, like "I don't mean to romanticize the student movements of the past." Actually, I don't have a big problem with doing a little bit of romanticizing if it helps to reclaim the decoloniz-ing power that these movements began to unleash before being set upon by the full force of state violence. That's particularly important when we try to come to terms with another face of this counterinsurgency: the way in which neoliberal politicians, pundits, and administrators have persistently and successfully *demeaned* student move-ments over the past five decades—for example, recasting collective struggles for redistribution and restructuring as the individual "grievances" of spoiled students (today's "snowflakes" are said to be an example of this)—as part of "an ideological project meant to tear down the web of insurgencies that activists have been demanding."[25]

24   Martha Biondi, *The Black Revolution on Campus* (Berkeley: University of California Press, 2012), p. 125.

25   Ferguson, *We Demand*, p. 68-69.

This way of telling the story nods towards the "historic" achievements of the Civil Rights Movement and student and youth activists of The Sixties—and even offers a sad shake of the head at the Kent State massacre—but then scorns today's supposedly coddled, whining students who are said to be nothing at all like those fine and righteous student activists of the past. Joe Biden gave voice to this position clearly, if not eloquently, while he was running for President: "The younger generation now tells me how tough things are. Give me a break. No, no, I have no empathy for it. Give me a break. Because here's the deal guys, we decided we were gonna change the world. And we did. We did. We finished the civil rights movement in the first stage. The women's movement came to be. So my message is, get involved."[26]

Let's think carefully in this context about something I have heard over and over about students in the US, including my CUNY students: that they are overcome by political apathy. Admittedly, with the rise of remarkable youth-led movements over the past decade, this has become a less common cliché and has been replaced, among some pundits, with the discourse of "whiny

26   Eve Peyser, "Biden Trashes Millennials in His Quest to Become Even Less Likable," *Vice* (January 12, 2018).

privileged students who want everything to be a safe space." But during the first decade that I was teaching, from the late 1990s into the 2000s, the hand-wringing consensus was that students in the US were by and large politically apathetic—not like the noble students of the past (well, the nonviolent ones, anyway).

We must refuse this version of the story, so carefully constructed by neoliberals in the 1980s and 90s, which claims that student movements combusted from within or ran out of steam, that students got tired of chanting and finally learned to be tolerant and trust the administrators, and that now everything is fine in any case. Let's hold on instead to the alternate story I have tried to tell: student activists striving for social change (in fact, students more generally) were violently and ruthlessly repressed, criminalized, surveilled, and demeaned, while also being systematically impoverished by student debt, for five decades, but have never stopped resisting.

This is also the context in which I have tried to understand a sentence I've been hearing from my students, with a few variations, since I started teaching at Kingsborough Community College in 2005. The majority of students at KCC are—to use the idiom of the administrators—among the most "under-served" in New York City. With the exception of a brief moment during the height of Occupy Wall Street in 2011,

I have yet to experience any sort of palpable political mobilization among the KCC student body. There are lots of reasons for this which are complex and structural, and also a variety of ways in which my students use the "weapons of the weak" to resist authority.[27] I love them for this, though sometimes, when they are aimed at me, I also gently curse them for it. But I have to believe at least some of this so-called "apathy" stems from the sentence I've heard from students again and again, repeated in different contexts and with different phrasings and accents but always coming back to the same simple declaration:

"Professor, anybody who has ever really tried to change things in this country got killed."

I can, of course, complicate this statement, but I can't tell them they are wrong. The context for this sense of tragic political analysis—which is quite different from apathy—is precisely the history of violence that I've outlined above.[28] A different narrative of this history—not

27 James Scott, *Weapons of the Weak: Everyday Forms of Peasant Resistance* (New Haven:Yale UP, 1985).

28 The key book for thinking about this legacy of political tragedy, coming out of the violent repression of anti-colonial revolutionary movements, is David Scott, *Omens of Adversity: Tragedy, Time, Memory, Justice* (Durham: Duke University Press, 2014).

one that leaves out the tragedy or the violence, but one that also includes the struggles for decolonization carried forward by student movements whose gains brought forth this violent reaction—has the potential to generate a different analysis.

This has been my main argument in this book: "multiculturalism" in its current institutional form is what we're left with when institutions reconfigure radical student demands seeking to transform the system into slogans that strengthen the university's "brand." Roderick Ferguson expresses it well: "Rather than a result of student demands, we might more accurately think of diversity offices as the administrative and bureaucratic response to those demands."[29] But this means that multiculturalism also contains traces of the original radical demands of the youth movements of the sixties and seventies: to open up the university, to wrench it from its settler colonial, white supremacist, and patriarchal capitalist origins, and to transform it into a place of radical democratic possibility. Those tasks remain utterly incomplete today.

Decolonizing multiculturalism, then, begins with the act of returning it to its radical roots.

29   Ferguson, *We Demand*, p. 26.

Chapter Seven

OVERTHROWING
AUSTERITY MULTICULTURALISM,
OR, YOU WON'T FIND
DECOLONIZATION ON THE
SYLLABUS

At the very end of Orhan Pamuk's novel *Snow*, we get to hear from Fazıl, a young political Islamist and budding sci-fi writer from the impoverished city of Kars in the northeast corner of Turkey. Fazıl's best friend, Necip, had been shot to death by soldiers before his eyes during an attempted political coup four years earlier. The book's first-person narrator—a novelist from Istanbul named Orhan who is visiting Kars and considering writing a book about those events—looks to Fazıl for some guidance on how he would want to be represented in such a novel:

> I turned back to Fazıl and asked him whether he knew now what he might want to say to my readers if ever I was to write a book set in Kars.
>
> "Nothing." His voice was determined.
>
> When he saw my face fall, he relented. "I did think of something, but you may not like it," he said. "If you write a book set in Kars and put me in it, I'd like to tell your readers not to believe anything you say about me, anything you say about any of us. No one could understand us from so far away."
>
> "But no one believes in that way what he reads in a novel," I said.
>
> "Oh, yes, they do," he cried. "If only to see themselves as wise and superior and humanistic, they need to think of us as sweet and funny, and convince themselves that they sympathize with the way we are and even love us. But if you would put in what I've

just said, at least your readers will keep a little room
for doubt in their minds."

I promised I would put what he'd said into
my novel.[1]

Fazıl is quick to recognize how privileged audiences often
want novels to act as risk-free (and commitment-free)
portals allowing them to "know" others—particularly
those others that they pay the police to keep far away
from their own communities. It may be that ordinarily,
"no one believes in that way what he reads in a novel."
But when it comes to novels that represent minoritized
communities for privileged readers, it's a different story:
they are "for educational purposes, racism and homo-
phobia and stuff."[2]

That last phrase comes from cultural critic Lauren
Michele Jackson, describing the phenomenon she calls
"The Anti-Racist Reading List." No doubt you've
encountered such lists, which have been around for
a long time but went viral in the wake of the popular uprisings following the police murder of George
Floyd in May 2020. They invariably include the sorts

1   Orhan Pamuk, *Snow*, translated by Maureen Freely (New York:
    Vintage, 2005), p. 426.

2   Lauren Michele Jackson, "What Is an Anti-Racist Reading List
    For?" *Vulture* (June 4, 2020).

of How-to-Be-an-Anti-Racist books that shot up the best-seller list that summer, especially the two that Jackson calls the "mac daddies" of the genre: Ibram X. Kendi's *How to Be an Antiracist* and Robin DiAngelo's *White Fragility*. But you'll also find plenty of literary works on these lists: Audre Lorde's *Sister Outsider*, James Baldwin's *The Fire Next Time*, Toni Morrison's *The Bluest Eye*, Ta-Nehisi Coates' *Between the World and Me*, Zora Neale Hurston's *Their Eyes Were Watching God*, Claudia Rankine's *Citizen*, and Frantz Fanon's *Black Skin, White Masks*, to name a few of the most prominent.

How could anyone quarrel with a list like this? After all, the average Anti-Racist Reading List includes some of the most brilliant and radical books of the past century. But the problem lies in the reading practice that the act of creating such a list encourages among its target audience—made up primarily of privileged white audiences seeking to be "enlightened" about racism—which Jackson describes acidly as the invitation "to read black art zoologically." Against the gooey mass of The Anti-Racism Reading List, which shoves novels, poetry, and memoirs into the same shapeless bag with how-to anti-racism readers and hands the whole thing over to privileged audiences seeking peak wokeness, Jackson provides a bracing alternative: "If you want to read a novel, read a damn novel, like it's a novel."

There's an important rhyme here between Pamuk and Jackson. Whether it's novels representing Kurdish characters for a primarily Turkish audience or novels representing African American characters for a primarily white audience, the dynamic is disturbingly similar. For privileged readers, the act of consuming such novels comes to seem like a positive action in and of itself. Reading sad stories about Black lives, white readers can "convince themselves that they sympathize with the way we are and even love us," just like the privileged readers of Orhan's book would be prepared to piously absorb, maybe even weep over, Fazıl's story. Then they can get on with their lives, with a little frisson of pleasure about their wokeness coupled with the unspoken but comforting thought that they won't ever have to live like (or close to) those people.

So why is it so hard to read a damn (multicultural) novel like it's a novel?

Austerity: The Malevolent Unicorn

One of the main culprits here is austerity multiculturalism. What do I mean by that? Let's start with the "austerity" part: simply put, we're all living in the age of fiscal austerity. The economist Mark Blyth defines this as "a form of voluntary deflation in which the economy adjusts through its reduction of wages, prices, and public spending to restore competitiveness, which is (supposedly) best achieved by cutting the state's budgets, debts, and deficits." This leads to increased "business confidence" that in turn leads to economic benefits for all: a rising tide that lifts all boats. In a nutshell, budget cuts—specifically cuts to wages, public spending, and public services—lead to growth. It is a simple and elegant solution. There's only one problem: it's completely and utterly wrong. Blyth, who unlike me is an economist and studies such things, says that the first time he encountered this claim for "austerity as a route to growth," his reaction was: "that's about as plausible as a unicorn with a bag of magic salt."[3]

That unicorn could be the mascot for the contemporary university. Particularly at public institutions, austerity is not just the dominant approach; it's the common

3   Mark Blyth, *Austerity: The History of a Dangerous Idea* (New York: Oxford University Press, 2013), p. ix-x, 2-3. Blyth has also made an entertaining video with the five-minute-version of his argument that's well worth watching; you can find it on YouTube. For other important recent work on austerity and the larger political and economic era of neoliberalism, see Wendy Brown, *In the Ruins of Neoliberalism: The Rise of Antidemocratic Politics in the West* (New York: Columbia University Press, 2019), as well as David Harvey, *A Brief History of Neoliberalism* (New York: Oxford University Press, 2007) and *The Anti-Capitalist Chronicles* (London: Pluto Press, 2020)—the latter can also be found as a podcast of the same name.

sense understanding of how things *must* work. For the average university administrator, austerity is like oxygen; folks like me who believe there might be an alternative are seen as the true unicorn seekers. The logic of austerity, which insists that the only way to create growth is via cuts, has become, not just the governing idea of fiscal policy, but the common sense understanding of how the world works.

The response to the COVID-19 pandemic has been the ultimate test case, and CUNY provides a useful example. During the Great Depression of the 1930s, policymakers, far from cutting public education budgets, invested heavily in the development of CUNY, seeing public education as crucial to economic recovery; in fact, three new CUNY campuses were opened during the darkest days of the Depression.[4] The COVID pandemic and its ensuing economic consequences could have easily inspired a similar decision to reinvest in public education precisely because it has so often been an engine of economic growth. We know, of course, what happened instead, at CUNY and elsewhere: programs cut, departments and campuses shuttered, massive layoffs

4   Jeanne Theoharis, Alan Aja, and Joseph Entin, "Spare CUNY, and Save the Education our Heroes Deserve," *City Limits* (May 13, 2020).

of precarious employees (increasingly, even tenure-track or tenured faculty are being fired), tuition and fees going up while funding for students goes down. As 2020 came to an end, higher education had lost at least a tenth of its labor force since the start of the pandemic; more than half a million college and university workers lost their jobs in just one year.[5]

There's magical thinking in the belief that such cuts will somehow lead to growth. There's also a deep cruelty at the heart of it, which makes the magical unicorn of austerity suddenly look like a much more malign creature. According to a 2019 study, roughly 48 percent of CUNY students suffer from food insecurity, 55 percent of CUNY students suffer from housing insecurity, and nearly 15 percent of CUNY students are or have been homeless while attending college.[6] And these numbers are from *before* the COVID-19 pandemic was ever thought of; they will be incalculably worse over the next few years.

5   Dan Bauman, "Colleges Have Shed a Tenth of Their Employees Since the Pandemic Began," *Chronicle of Higher Education* (November 10, 2020).

6   Ben Chapman, "Thousands of CUNY Students Experience Homelessness and Food Insecurity, Report Says," *New York Daily News* (27 March 2019).

But when it comes to austerity, the cruelty is part of the point. Advocates of austerity are fond of talking about the need for "discipline"—usually in reference to the same poor communities most likely to be the objects of discipline in the form of direct state violence. But there's a way in which the perverse logic of "cuts lead to growth" allows the perpetrators of austerity to present themselves as healers rather than butchers ("this will hurt a little, but it's good for you!"). The final lines of Fred L. Joiner's poem "Austerity" capture this perfectly:

> . . . The language
> of cutting is a subtle lexicon, always
> sounds kinder, gentler, than the trill blade
> under the tongue of our economy's math. Soft,
>   sayings
> like *human scale*, like *rightsizing*,
> like *achieving efficiencies*
> hide the blade, hide the murder
> that pen and protocol make, masked.[7]

7   Fred L. Joiner, "Austerity," *Delaware Poetry Review* 8.1 (2016). In an interview, Joiner talked about how his own experience of being laid off ("downsized") from his job helped make him a poet. See Maria Hollenhorst, "A Poet's Take on 'Austerity,'" *Marketplace* (December 4, 2020).

Just Do Much More with Much Less!: The Curricula of Austerity

So what's the connection between economic austerity and multiculturalism? After all, austerity is all about cutting back and tightening belts, while multiculturalism seems to be all about adding and multiplying: more cultures, more variety, more diversity. In practice, however, one of the most damaging effects of austerity, especially at public universities, has been upon the stuff of learning itself. Michael Fabricant and Stephen Brier's comprehensive and bruising study *Austerity Blues: Fighting for the Soul of Public Higher Education* describes what they call "the curricula of austerity." It's created through the constant demand upon public universities "to do more with less"—the inevitable extension of austerity's mantra of "cuts lead to growth." "Growth" is of course best measured by "productivity," which in turn require "metrics" and "rubrics" (those favorite terms of university administrators). For K-12 education, the metric of choice is high-stakes testing; for higher education, it's "time-to-degree" and graduation rates.[8]

8   Michael Fabricant and Stephen Brier, *Austerity Blues: Fighting for the Soul of Public Higher Education* (Baltimore: Johns Hopkins University Press, 2016), p. 104-08.

This is how you *literally* produce growth through cuts: dilute the curriculum to manufacture more graduates faster. So public universities in several states have simply reduced the number of credits needed to graduate: one way to do more with less is to do less (learning) with more (students). In other cases, there have pushes to eliminate "low-productivity" degrees (including history, political science, philosophy, and foreign languages and literatures). Fabricant and Brier sum up the grim landscape: "The drive to impose efficiencies has resulted in the elimination of courses or whole disciplines not clearly aligned with concrete market needs and, thus, declared unproductive."[9] Indeed, an increasing number of state legislatures have suggested that the era of public investment in colleges and universities that offer a humanities education to working class students may simply be over and done with.

The effects of austerity are unevenly borne. This is the clear injustice of austerity logic, by which public spending must be reduced to prevent it from "crowding out" private investment. The resultant cuts to public services are suffered mostly by those at the bottom of the economic ladder, who actually *use* those public services

---

9   Fabricant and Brier, *Austerity Blues*, p. 241.

(or used to use them, before they were cut or eliminated altogether). Meanwhile, those at the top, who get richer from the dividends of private investments, are totally unaffected by these cuts, since they would never dream of rubbing shoulders with the riffraff riding the subway, relying on state-funded medical care, or—heaven forfend!—sending their children to public schools.

So too with the curricula of austerity, intended primarily for working class students, and particularly those from racially minoritized communities—precisely the communities that had traditionally been excluded from public universities before the struggles of the Civil Rights Movement and of anti-racist student movements began to desegregate these universities. As with individuals, so with institutions: the rich get richer, the poor get austerity. While public schools have been facing "growth friendly fiscal consolidation" for more than a decade, federal payments and entitlements to Ivy League schools increased to $41.59 billion between 2010 and 2015. Today, the annual amount of federal money received by any individual Ivy is greater than the *total annual amount* received by many states for public education.[10] So we grow.

10 See "Ivy League, Inc.: U.S. Taxpayer Subsidies, Tax-Breaks and Federal Payments into the Ivy League Colleges, Fiscal Years 2010-2015," *Open the Books Oversight Report*, March 2017.

The Diversity Requirement, or Dial "M" for Multiculturalism!

So when I talk about "austerity multiculturalism," I'm referring to the simple fact that austerity is the air we breathe today (which is perhaps why so many can't breathe). But I mean something more specific as well. Not surprisingly, given how nicely institutional multiculturalism fits the demands of the neoliberal university, there are some particular ways that multiculturalism has evolved in response to the call to "do more with less" which is the golden rule of austerity.

Take, for example, the "diversity requirement." Literally: if you're an undergraduate at almost any college or university, you'll have to take one or two or three or *possibly even four* classes that meet the "diversity requirement" to be able to graduate. For example, the University of Southern California's website informs us that its diversity requirement "is designed to provide undergraduate students with the background knowledge and analytical skills necessary to understand and respect differences between groups of people," since "students will increasingly need to grapple with issues arising from different dimensions of human diversity such as age, disability, ethnicity, gender, language, race, religion, sexual orientation, and social class." See, you've learned a lesson before you even signed up for a class: "differences between groups of people" apparently need to be "grappled" with! But fulfilling this lofty goal won't cause students to break a sweat: despite the rhetorical fanfare, it turns out that USC's diversity requirement "can be met by passing any one course carrying the designation 'm' for multiculturalism."

Meanwhile, at Villanova University, students are required to take at least two courses designated as "diversity" classes, because "learning to see through the eyes of other peoples and cultures is essential to becoming a citizen of the world." Those two classes are made to carry a very large burden, though, since they are asked to cover three massive areas:

> **Diversity 1:** Courses that focus on populations (often named as non-dominant, minority, or impoverished groups) in the US or Western Europe, and the systems or mechanisms that give rise to the experiences of power, privilege, and marginalization.

> **Diversity 2:** Courses that focus on women's experiences and/or highlight the relationship between gender, culture, and power.

> **Diversity 3:** Courses that focus on the culture, economics, politics or ecology of societies and nations other than those of Western Europe and the United

States and that emphasize power, privilege, and marginalization or a critical analysis of how these cultures define and express themselves.

At Kent State University, where I started my teaching career—as you might recall, back in 1999, a KSU administrator rejoiced that my newly designed postcolonial literature course would fulfill the diversity requirement—the stated purpose of this requirement "is to help educate students to live in a world of diverse communities, many of which are becoming increasingly permeated with cultural and ideological differences." For this, two courses will suffice: one addressing "domestic (US) issues" and one addressing "global issues." Closer to home, at Hunter College in the CUNY system, students must take four (!) classes to meet the "Pluralism and Diversity Requirement"; however, one of these is to focus on Europe, alongside Non-European societies (one course); African Americans, Asian Americans, Latino Americans, or Native Americans (one course); and women and/or issues of gender or sexual orientation (one course).

You get the idea. Just to be clear: in attacking the insufficiency at the heart of these administrative requirements, I have no intention of providing ammunition to the loathsome right-wing bottom-feeders who attack such diversity requirements or courses in the name of "declining standards." That's just racist nonsense. But what I am concerned with is how the "diversity requirement" fits perfectly into today's curricula of austerity. The struggle to decolonize the university that was fought by a generation of student movements, and is still being fought today, has been not just co-opted but actually turned into a quantifiable metric. "If we want to turn out an effective global citizen," the equation goes, "how can we produce one in the quickest, least costly manner?" Well, that required Intro to Sociology class you need to take anyway? We'll slap an "M" for Multiculturalism on that and you're good to go!

One-of-Eachism, or, Don't Worry, We'll Just Add It to the Syllabus!

We're ready to return to that question of why it's so hard to read a damn (multicultural) novel like it's a novel. For the same austerity logic I've been describing can all too easily get repeated, even by those of us totally dedicated to decolonizing the university, in the most fundamental pedagogical act of all: writing a syllabus. I'm thinking specifically of a syllabus for a course that might earn that "M for Multiculturalism" rubric—for example, a World Literature class.

The rules of austerity multiculturalism mean that teaching a class like this carries a burden: after all, this might be the one and only course a student will ever take dedicated to "global issues"! That burden is then shifted onto the literary texts—usually novels—that get taught in such a class. Since a World Literature class is expected to provide students with a "global" experience, certain books in turn get called upon to bear the representative burden for a particular nation ("Indian literature"), race ("African-American literature"), culture ("literatures of the Asian diaspora"), and/or religious community ("literatures of the Islamic world").

This is the reading practice that I call "one-of-eachism": a way of reading in which an individual book is given a representational status, asked to stand in for a particular country or culture or group. If you want to achieve the "multi" in "multiculturalism" within the sped up and slimmed down curricula of austerity, after all, there's really no time for more than one specimen of any particular culture in any particular class. One-of-eachism, then, is the process by which an individual literary work, given the limiting context necessitated by austerity multiculturalism, comes to be considered not as a novel from India but as *the* novel from India—or, in other cases, *the* novel from the Caribbean, or *the* novel from Africa, or *the* novel from "the Islamic World," and so on. This is rarely a conscious or premeditated move; rather, it's the inevitable result of being forced to obey the logic of austerity—do more with less—while still meeting the "diversity requirement."

The further step in this process is that these literary works generally wind up being read in a manner that is more sociological than literary in nature— "zoological" reading, as Lauren Michele Jackson calls it. This means that a "multicultural" novel is not only called upon to represent the national literary tradition from which it comes; it's often called upon to represent an entire nation (or, usually in the case of African literature, an entire continent); or the entirety of a gendered existence; or indeed, the collective experiences of whole communities of "non-dominant, minority, or impoverished groups." No wonder it becomes impossible to read a damn novel like it's a novel!

Let's stay with the example of a World Literature course, both because it's the one I'm most familiar with and also because such courses are the building blocks of austerity multiculturalism. World Lit classes are built on the notion that literary texts can move freely across borders and boundaries, including linguistic ones, landing happily at the feet of American students. Alexander Beecroft, in his fascinating book *An Ecology of World Literature*, describes this as the belief in a "global literary ecology"—that is, a "literary circulation that truly knows no borders." Beecroft coins the term "global literature" to describe particular contemporary texts "designed to narrate shared global experiences in a linguistic register freed from slang and ambiguity in order to be translated as seamlessly as possible from one language to another."[11]

This global literature is then delivered to an English-speaking audience through a form of translation practice that aims for "invisibility."[12] That is, rather than rendering a text into English in a way that reminds the reader that it was translated from a different language, the goal is to make the translation as smooth

11   Alexander Beecroft, *An Ecology of World Literature: From Antiquity to the Present Day* (New York: Verso, 2015), p. 33, 281.

12   I'm borrowing the term from Lawrence Venuti's *The Translator's Invisibility: A History of Translation* (New York: Routledge, 1995). For a study of the way that translation in fact leaves a very *visible* legacy on "world literature," see María Constanza Guzmán, *Gregory Rabassa's Latin American Literature: A Translator's Visible Legacy* (Lewisburg: Bucknell University Press. 2010).

and readable as possible. That means making it seem immediately familiar to an English-language audience, rather than calling attention to idioms or grammatical constructions or other points of difference in the original language that would otherwise provide sticking points. Of course, these sticking points are precisely the sorts of things that are meant to be discussed in a literature classroom.

When this becomes the standard for all books translated into English, what you wind up with is an array of novels from very different places, written in very different languages and using very different styles, that wind up sounding very similar and offering very similar reading experiences. The end result is that for students in a World Literature class, "the literature by a woman in Palestine begins to resemble, in the feel of its prose, something by a man in Taiwan."[13] These global texts, smoothly translated so they can be effortlessly placed alongside books by Anglophone "world writers" who hail mostly from former British colonies, are the bread and butter of World Literature classes in the United States.

---

13   Gayatri Chakravorty Spivak, *Outside in the Teaching Machine* (New York: Routledge, 1993), p. 182.

Listen, That Nation Is Speaking!

This whole process in turn creates a handful of writers—many writing in English, a few skillfully translated—who have achieved the title of "world writers," and accordingly are omnipresent on World Literature syllabi. Take the example with whom I began this chapter: Orhan Pamuk. Pamuk had begun to bear the title of "world writer" even before he was awarded the Nobel Prize for Literature in 2006; the enthusiastic reception of his books in English translation—particularly *Snow*, which became a bestseller in the US and UK after it was translated in 2004—no doubt played a role in his winning the Nobel at a relatively young age. The American reception of Pamuk's work is symptomatic of how "world writers" get read in the classrooms of austerity multiculturalism. At the heart of this reception is the demand that such writers become *the* representative voices for their nation or region. In Pamuk's case, Western readers, reviewers, and teachers of his work have generally treated him as the representative voice of Turkey. Needless to say, reviewers of his translated novels can rarely resist the chance to compare Pamuk's prose to the sweetness of Turkish delight or his plots to the complexity of "Oriental" carpets.

A sentence from Canadian novelist Margaret Atwood's review of *Snow* in *The New York Times Book Review* is a perfect example. In *Snow*, Atwood assures us, Pamuk "is narrating his country into being."[14] This would no doubt come as a surprise to Pamuk, as well as to countless other Turkish writers over the past century who very likely believe they may also have played some part in this process of narrating the nation, but it gives a good indication of the pressure placed on the "world writer" to represent his or her (generally, *his*) nation for a Western audience. Atwood's comment is weirdly similar to the praise granted to Salman Rushdie's *Midnight's Children* when that novel was published in 1981. Another Canadian writer, Clark Blaise, again writing for *The New York Times Book Review*, proclaimed that Rushdie's novel "sounds like a continent finding its voice."[15] This is intended as a compliment, like Atwood's sentence, but completely ignores the fact that Rushdie's novel comes out of a long and important tradition of South Asian literature, particularly literature in languages other than English. When it comes to "world writers,"

14 Margaret Atwood, "Headscarves to Die For," *The New York Times Book Review* (August 15, 2004).

15 Clark Blaise, "A Novel of India's Coming of Age," *The New York Times Book Review* (April 19, 1981).

however, if you're not writing in English—or, as in the case of Pamuk, unless you are translated skillfully into English—you don't really exist.[16]

There is also a related but different burden that weighs upon Pamuk and Rushdie, since both are generally described in the US and Europe as "Muslim writers." This is an identity that has nothing to do with the question of actual belief, of course, and like the identity of "representative" national writer, is one conferred and reinforced from the outside (you don't generally see Margaret Atwood or Ernest Hemingway or Günter Grass or John Updike described as "Christian writers"). Shortly before Pamuk won the Nobel Prize, one critic wrote: "Critically renowned, translated into more than thirty languages, Pamuk is surpassing Salman Rushdie as the world's pre-eminent Muslim writer."[17] Again, this assertion would no doubt come as a surprise not only to Pamuk, who is not apt to refer to himself as a "Muslim writer," but also to literally thousands of

16   Aijaz Ahmad said as much in his response to Blaise's review of Rushdie's novel: "as if one has no voice if one does not speak in English." *In Theory: Classes, Nations, Literatures* (New York: Verso, 1992), p. 98.

17   Randy Boyagoda, "Identity Crisis." *The Walrus* (July 2005).

writers working in Arabic, Persian, Urdu, Indonesian, Turkish, and countless other languages.

What is meant by statements like this, of course, is that Rushdie and Pamuk are the pre-eminent Muslim writers *for English-language readers.* The representational burden that comes with this role is greater even than that of being the sole national spokesperson on a World Literature syllabus, especially coming from Western readers seeking a guide to understanding "the Islamic world"—a task that has, for obvious reasons, seemed more urgent for such readers since September 2001. Pamuk's novel *Snow* in particular, since it takes as one of its central subjects the Turkish "headscarf controversy" and engages with larger questions of gender and Islam, political violence, and fundamentalism (both religious and secular), has been asked to play this explanatory role by many Western readers.

Snow is therefore a staple of the multicultural classroom. That's not a criticism of the novel, which, in my expert critical opinion as a literature professor, is fucking amazing. What we have here is the same problem as that which accompanies the Anti-Racist Reading List: *Snow* gets taught so often in World Literature classes not because of what it actually is or does or says, but because of what austerity multiculturalism wants it to do: "represent the other!"

"One-of-eachism," the fundamental principle of multicultural syllabus-making, means that when it comes to a "world writer" like Pamuk, the jump is from being read as a writer from Turkey to coming to be placed in the position of *the* Turkish writer. Rushdie's *Midnight's Children* becomes, in such a context, an introduction to India, and *Snow* becomes, depending on the need, an introduction to Turkey, to the Middle East, or perhaps even to that massive and massively misrepresented entity called "the Islamic world." The demand upon such novels could be summarized somewhat crudely but not inaccurately as: tell us about India, or Turkey, or the Middle East, or Africa, or the Islamic world, so that we can better understand it.

"Turkey's Most Famous Novelist (Pronounced OR-han PAH-mook)"

But surely there's no harm in reading literature to better understand other places and other people, right? Isn't this multiculturalism at its naïve but well-intentioned best?

The famous war criminal George W. Bush would agree. In fact, he used this same sort of multiculturalist logic to defend the invasion and occupation of Iraq, arguably the greatest crime of the twenty-first century (so far). On a visit to Turkey in June 2004 to drum up support for the continuing occupation of Iraq, Bush

ended a speech on "democracy and freedom" by referring to "the Turkish writer Orhan Pamuk." In Bush's
account, Pamuk's work "has been a bridge between cultures," allowing us "to realize that other peoples in other
continents and civilizations are exactly like you." That
sentiment may sound heartwarming, but the chilling
geopolitical consequences become clear in Bush's final
sentence: "in their need for hope, in their desire for peace,
in their right to freedom, the peoples of the Middle East
are exactly like you and me. Their birthright of freedom
has been denied for too long. And we will do all in our
power to help them find the blessings of liberty."[18]

In the name of such multicultural oneness, Iraq
was destroyed.

As an intrepid *Boston Globe* reporter wrote a few
months later, "Who knew George W. Bush had a taste
for Turkish literature? Yet there he was in Istanbul last
June, quoting Turkey's most famous novelist, Orhan
Pamuk (pronounced OR-han PAH-mook)."[19] And forever after, English professors who had marched in the

18   "President Bush Discusses Democracy, Freedom From Turkey,"
     Official White House Press Release (June 29, 2004).

19   Mark Feeney, "Orhan Pamuk Sees the World: The Turkish
     Writer's Work Serves as a Literary Bridge between East and
     West," *Boston Globe* (October 11, 2004).

streets against the war returned to their classrooms, to teach Pamuk's work as "a bridge between cultures."

We literature professors, for all our good intentions, have some reckoning to do. "Literary studies within US universities," writes Jodi Melamed, "plays a number of roles." One is, quite simply, to contribute to the self-care of elites, endowing them with a sense of being "part of a multinational group of enlightened multicultural global citizens." In a more sinister vein, literary studies also acquaints these elites-in-training "with representations of dispossessed populations, preparing them for their role in global civilizing/disqualifying regimes."[20]

On the local level, as Hazel Carby has shown, that means reading sad stories of Black lives while assenting to (and sometimes actively taking part in) structural violence against Black communities. Carby noted the consequences of this dynamic in a brilliant series of essays written in the early 1990s, at the moment when neoliberal multiculturalism was establishing its dominance. From one angle, the publishing explosion of Black women's fiction that was "a major influence in multicultural curriculum development" could only be

20   Jodi Melamed, *Represent and Destroy: Rationalizing Violence in the New Racial Capitalism* (Minneapolis: University of Minnesota Press, 2011), p. 158-59.

celebrated; after all, the demand to bring the voices of Black women writers into the classroom had come originally from radical student movements pushing for programs in Black studies and women's studies.

But Carby shows what happened once these works were subjected to the workings of institutional multiculturalism. Texts by Black women writers, far from being allowed to exist in a context where they could have a transformative effect upon knowledge production, became simply "a way of gaining knowledge of the 'other': a knowledge that appears to satisfy and replace the desire to challenge existing frameworks of segregation." She draws the painful conclusion in the form of a question: "Have we, as a society, successfully eliminated the desire for achieving integration through political agitation for civil rights and opted instead for knowing each other through cultural texts?"[21] Twenty years on, it's clear that the answer, sadly, is: yes.

Reading Black women's texts in the context provided by institutional multiculturalism, in other words, becomes not the inspiration for true anti-racist political

---

21   The essay from which this quote is taken was originally published as "The Multicultural Wars," in *Radical History Review* 54.7 (1992); it was republished as "The Multicultural Wars, Part One" as a chapter of Carby's book *Cultures in Babylon: Black Britain and African America* (New York: Verso, 1999), p. 253.

work but a *substitution* for such work. The Anti-Racism Reading List too often works in a similar way: "Black Lives Matter" can easily become, for privileged white readers, "Black lives make great reading matter!"

But what about the global level? After all, some of these elites-in-training will someday have to help decide which populations need to be bombed into oblivion in order for them to "find the blessings of liberty," as George W. put it. Cue the World Literature class. Teaching global literature to suit the purposes of neoliberalism simply means expanding the institutional approach taken towards "multicultural literature" (generally understood to mean American literature not written by white people) in order to include "non-Western literature." The popularity and usefulness of the category of "global literature" arises precisely "out of its promise to make non-Western cultures readily available." More specifically, reading "global literature" prepares students for their future role in US imperialism, by assuring them that "what we need to know about 'them' is that they are much like us, at least those eligible for global multicultural citizenship."[22] A recent piece about Pamuk's *Snow*, in which the author suggests that the book "predicted" both the events of 9/11 and

22   Melamed, *Represent and Destroy*, p. 161.

also the election of Donald Trump (as though a novel about Turkey had nothing better to do than make predictions about US politics), sums it up: "Orhan Pamuk's *Snow*: A Book About 'Other' People—and Therefore Us."[23]

We've seen this show before. This is diversity management—the process by which difference is prevented from making a difference—on a global scale. More specifically, as Angela Davis reminds us, diversity management ensures that "difference doesn't make any difference, if only we acquire knowledge about it." As a critic of institutional multiculturalism, but also as a Black woman writer herself and thus an *object* of multicultural diversity management, Davis spells out the consequences: "If our difference is understood, consumed, and 'digested,' we simultaneously can be different and perform 'as if' we really were middle-class, straight white males."[24] Or, in the case of world writers, "as if" they were American or European—that is, "regular"—writers.

23   Sam Jordison, "Orhan Pamuk's *Snow*: A Book About 'Other' People—and Therefore Us," *The Guardian* (March 20, 2018).

24   Angela Davis, "Gender, Class, and Multiculturalism: Rethinking 'Race' Politics," in *Mapping Multiculturalism*, ed. Avery F. Gordon and Christopher Newfield (Minneapolis: University of Minnesota Press, 1996), p. 46.

Ultimately, *that's* what's most damaging about austerity multiculturalism's ethos of "they're really just like
us," enabled by the "one-of-eachism" imposed on literary texts from the non-West. That supposed "sameness"
is not liberalism's avowed leveling process of achieving political equality, nor is it neoliberalism's promised
economic rising tide that lifts all boats. It's the leveling
imposed by the falling bombs that flatten "their" houses
to make them more like "us."

Some Other Things That World Literature Can Do

It should be said, for all you lovers of literature who
might be smarting a bit by now, that many of the harsh-
est critics of multicultural literary studies are themselves literary critics. Jodi Melamed teaches mostly in an
English department. So does Lauren Michele Jackson.
Angela Davis and Hazel Carby don't, but the former
started out as a student of French literature and the latter
as a high-school English teacher, and both have produced a number of works that would be recognizable
as literary studies. Aijaz Ahmad, responsible for incisive
critiques of the demand that "world literature" speak
English, spent much of his life teaching in literature
departments. So did Edward Said, the great critic of

cultural imperialism. Even Ngũgĩ wa Thiong'o, author of "On the Abolition of the English Department," is today a Distinguished Professor of English (among other titles) at the University of California at Irvine.[25]

I'm not playing "gotcha!" here. I teach in an English department myself. In fact, I've spent the better part of my life happily teaching literature. In the process of writing this book, I took part in a webcast for the "Decolonize That!" series, together with Bhakti Shringarpure (the series editor), Grégory Pierrot (who wrote the fantastic book *Decolonize Hipsters*), and Sophia Azeb (one of the brilliant organizers of the "More than Diversity" movement at the University of Chicago).[26] At a certain point off camera, we started talking about the strange fact that all of us, somehow, had wound up in English departments.

There are some boring institutional explanations for why so many would-be decolonizers can be found in English departments, even though many of us would readily agree that literary studies has too often played a

25 Ngũgĩ wa Thiong'o, "On the Abolition of the English Department," *Homecoming: Essays* (London: Heinemann, 1972).

26 "Decolonize That 4: No, It's NOT on the Syllabus" (October 23, 2020). See also Bhakti Shringarpure, "Notes on Fake Decolonization," *Africa Is a Country* (December 18, 2020).

doleful role in institutional multiculturalism. But here's the good news: we don't *have* to teach world literature solely as a way to prove that "we're all the same, really." There are a lot of other things that literature can do.

In fact, there has never been a time when literature was *not* a key part of creating radical political imaginaries, including within movements for decolonization. Re-activating radical literary study is thus an absolutely necessary aspect of decolonizing multiculturalism. And there's more good news: doing something as simple (and joyful) as following Jackson's exhortation to "read a novel like it's a damn novel" is the first step here.

One of our best guides for this is Barbara Harlow's 1987 book *Resistance Literature*. Written at precisely the moment when institutional multiculturalism was coming into its own, it provides a radical alternative for how to think about world literature, and really about *literature* more generally. It focuses on "literature that emerged significantly as part of the organized national liberation struggles and resistance movements in Africa, Latin America, and the Middle East."[27] For Harlow, literary

---

27 Barbara Harlow, *Resistance Literature* (New York: Methuen, 1987), p. xvii. Harlow's work has been carried on brilliantly by Anna Bernard: see her forthcoming book *Decolonizing Literature: An Introduction* (Cambridge: Polity Press, 2023).

texts from South Africa or Nicaragua or Palestine aren't guides to "knowing" those places, or even just descriptions of the struggles there; they are crucial creative *contributions* to the ongoing liberation struggles in each of those places. Reading and studying resistance literature, then, creates a different sort of responsibility: not just learning passively from these texts but engaging with them actively, as an act of solidarity.

It's no coincidence that Harlow borrows the term "resistance literature" from the Palestinian revolutionary writer Ghassan Kanafani, and that she shares Ngũgĩ's basic rule for literary studies: in the context of revolution, there are really only two kinds of literature—the literature of oppression and the literature of liberation.[28] Sadly, it's also not a coincidence that *Resistance Literature* is currently out of print. Let's get it back into circulation; we need it.

So am I saying that it's just a matter of putting some of this resistance literature on the syllabus? Well, a World Literature class that featured a few of the writers that Barbara Harlow wrote about—Kanafani, Ngũgĩ,

28 Harlow, *Resistance Literature*, p. 2, 9. See Ghassan Kanafani, *Literature of Resistance in Occupied Palestine: 1948-1966* (Beirut: Institute for Arab Research, 1982) and Ngũgĩ wa Thiong'o, "Literature in Schools," in *Writers in Politics* (London: Heinemann, 1981).

Bessie Head, Roque Dalton, Ruth First, Sahar Khalifeh, Ernesto Cardinal—would certainly be a step in the right direction. But it isn't quite so simple. One reason is that the context of austerity limits us everywhere we turn; your associate dean will be sure to tell you that adding new and different writers just isn't fiscally prudent, and anyway, it's hard to make a case for Bessie Head or Ghassan Kanafani as "market friendly." But more fundamentally, as we've seen, pursuing "diversity" simply through the act of addition won't get us to a decolonized university. The only real rule for getting there is the one that Fanon spelled out decades ago: "shake the worm-eaten foundations of the edifice."[29]

"A Creature Which Would Be Impossible If It Did Not Exist"

That's a tall order, so one thing decolonization demands is the creation of new political imaginaries. After all, even "austerity" itself is just a story—a unicorn with a bag of magic salt—that we've all been forced to live in. That's why when the late great Mark Fisher talked about our era as the age of "capitalist realism," he understood capitalist realism not as an ideology or a set of rules,

---

29 Frantz Fanon, *Black Skin, White Masks*, translated by Richard Philcox (New York: Grove, 2008), p. xv.

but as a more insidious thing: "a pervasive *atmosphere* . . . acting as a kind of invisible barrier constraining thought and action."[30] It's Margaret Thatcher's bone-dry statement about capitalism—"there is no alternative"—taken from the realm of wishful thinking to that of "fact." And so we get the neoliberal university, where, we are constantly assured, cutting budgets, programs, and people leads to growth, where less is more, and where "multicultural diversity"—whose very definition implies variety and proliferation—is best achieved via austerity.

This is the field of struggle where English professors can, maybe, begin to redeem ourselves. Literature—especially those brilliant texts that too often wind up getting imprisoned in "multicultural" classes like World Literature—is all about proliferation. Literature is also quite good at reminding us of the power inherent in stories, including the stories told to keep us in our places—the kinds of stories that make up capitalist realism, for example. And literature is *really* good at getting us to question what should count as "realistic" in the first place. This is particularly important, because austerity gets away with its magical thinking by insisting that it's the only realistic option. That's where we can

30   Mark Fisher, *Capitalist Realism: Is There No Alternative?* (London Zer0 Books, 2009), p. 16.

attack capitalist realism, since "what counts as 'realistic,' what seems possible at any point in the social field, is defined by a series of political determinations."[31] And political determinations, in turn, depend on political imagination.

All this means that reading literature doesn't have to take the place of working for political liberation, and literary study doesn't have to play the role of neoliberal helpmeet that it too often does in today's university. That's the other side of Jodi Melamed's argument, since like me (and maybe you), she loves literature and what literature can do. What she describes as the "roots" of "a race-radical tradition" that has tirelessly opposed racial capitalism can be "readily found in literary texts themselves (as compared to literary studies discourses)."[32] Again, it's a matter of returning to those roots—which is the very definition of radicalism, after all.

We've come back, via the long road, to the question of reading a novel like it's a damn novel. That's the last thing austerity multiculturalism wants us to do, especially with "world writers," who are only supposed to be there in the first place to help create better diversity managers.

31   Fisher, *Capitalist Realism*, p. 16-17.

32   Melamed, *Represent and Destroy*, p. 4.

That's why Salman Rushdie's *Midnight's Children* is such a useful text for austerity multiculturalism—you can teach the whole history of India with just one book! (Somewhere, an administrator is gleefully cancelling a "redundant" South Asian history class.) Granted, it's a long one, so we understand if you don't ask students to read the whole thing—that works for us!

There's only one problem. *Midnight's Children* is a great novel, and great novels don't cooperate. Don't get me wrong—Rushdie's novel isn't an example of resistance literature, in Harlow's sense; neither, for that matter, is Pamuk's *Snow.* But when you read it like a novel, *Midnight's Children* still has the power to interrupt the workings of austerity multiculturalism.

For one thing, it throws at us one of the most unreliable narrators you will ever meet. Saleem Sinai is transparently, even proudly, unreliable, gleefully changing dates and happily contradicting himself. For another, the novel anticipates and short-circuits the way austerity multiculturalism wants it to be read. In an essay written a few years after the novel was published, Rushdie described the desire for *Midnight's Children* "to be the history, even the guidebook, which it was never meant to be," and the subsequent disappointment of readers who approached it this way and then, upon finding all the things that were "left out," could only condemn it as an "inadequate reference book or encyclopedia."[33] But thanks to the form of the novel itself—starting with Saleem's unreliability—*Midnight's Children* invites us to question of our very sense of what counts as an "adequate" historical narrative in this first place, especially when it comes to the story of how a post-colonial nation came to be.

Take one episode spun out by Saleem early in the novel: the tragic narrative of Mian Abdullah, "The Hummingbird." The Hummingbird, in Saleem's account, was largely responsible for "the optimism epidemic" of 1942 that swept up Saleem's grandfather, among others, by presenting an alternative within the South Asian Muslim community to the separatist vision of Muhammad Ali Jinnah. This separatist vision was one that Jinnah shared with the British colonizers, resulting ultimately in the establishment of the states of East and West Pakistan (today's Bangladesh and Pakistan), a partition that continues to bleed today.

The Hummingbird himself is a professional conjurer (*Midnight's Children* is full of magicians) who, in the words of the popular press, "rose from the famous magicians' ghetto in Delhi to become the hope of India's hundred

---

33 Salman Rushdie, *Imaginary Homelands: Essays and Criticism 1981-1991* (London: Granta, 1991), p. 25.

million Muslims." He gained his nickname through his habit of continuously "humming in a strange way, neither musical nor unmusical, but somehow mechanical, the hum of an engine or a dynamo." Mian Abdullah was, in other words, "a creature which would be impossible if it did not exist," as Saleem declares.[34]

The assassination of Mian Abdullah—perhaps at the hands of Jinnah's supporters, perhaps at the hands of British agents (there were too many suspects, since he had too many enemies)—puts a sudden end to the optimism epidemic. His death, according to Saleem, closes down a movement that might have been part of a larger popular revolt against communalism and partition. The murder, refracted through a whole series of narrators, contains the same "impossibility" as the existence of the Hummingbird himself (including the intervention of hundreds of street dogs, drawn by the Hummingbird's high-pitched humming as he tries to defend himself, who attack and kill the assassins). Yet Saleem insists upon its historical accuracy: "If you don't believe me, check. Find out about Mian Abdullah and his Convocations. Discover how we've swept his story under the carpet."[35]

34   Salman Rushdie, *Midnight's Children: A Novel* (New York: Penguin, 1991), p. 39, 46.

35   Rushdie, *Midnight's Children*, p. 49.

Assiduous critics have done just this, but with little success.[36] No real-life Mian Abdullah appears to exist, and accordingly, historical parallels have had to be offered. But the search for the actual and factual existence of the Hummingbird takes us away from our primary work as teachers and students and readers of literature. "Sometimes legends make reality," Saleem tells us, in the midst of spinning out the story of the Hummingbird.[37] There was an alternative to Partition, a popular movement that might have changed history, and it was prevented from doing so. How does a novelist tell the story of that which has *not* happened?

That's the true conjuring that literature can perform—bringing lost possibilities from the past into the present. If we pay attention, literature can remind us that the world we have before us didn't *have* to turn out this way. There have always been alternatives. Decolonization is one of them. We just need to remember it, (re)imagine it, and then fight to make it real.

36 For one of the finest attempts, see Anne C. Hegerfeldt, *Lies that Tell the Truth: Magic Realism Seen through Contemporary Fiction from Britain* (Amsterdam: Rodopi, 2005).

37 Rushdie, *Midnight's Children*, p. 47.

DECOLONIZATION MEANS THE END OF THE WORLD [THAT'S THE GOOD NEWS]

At whatever level we study it—individual encounters, a change of name for a sports club, the guest list at a cocktail party, members of a police force or the board of directors of a state or private bank—decolonization is quite simply the substitution of one "species" of mankind by another . . . . In actual fact, proof of success lies in a social fabric that has been changed inside out.

—Frantz Fanon, *The Wretched of the Earth*[1]

"What can you do?"
"Start!"
"Start what?"
"The only thing in the world worth starting: the end of the world, for heaven's sake."

—Aimé Césaire, *Notebook of a Return to My Native Land*[2]

If you've skipped to the end in your impatience to find the simple solution for decolonizing multiculturalism, I'm afraid you're going to be disappointed. My guiding

1   Frantz Fanon, *The Wretched of the Earth*, translated by Richard Philcox (New York: Grove, 2004), p. 1.

2   Aimé Césaire, *Notebook of a Return to My Native Land*, translated by Mireille Rosello with Annie Pritchard (New York: Bloodaxe, 1995), p. 98, quoted in Frantz Fanon, *Black Skin, White Masks*, translated by Richard Philcox (New York: Grove, 2008), p. 76.

spirit, Frantz Fanon, began his first book, *Black Skin, White Masks*, with the declaration: "I'm not the bearer of absolute truths." And if *he* wasn't, then I'm sure as hell not.

"I honestly think, however," Fanon continued, "it's time some things were said."[3] Me too. Just saying them, or writing them, will never be enough. But we ended that last chapter on the question of the imagination—specifically, the political imagination—and if this book is to mean anything, I want us to be able to better imagine decolonization. Multiculturalism, not as it currently exists but as it might be made to become, is one important space where we can begin to imagine, and thus create, that decolonized "social fabric" for which Fanon spent his life fighting (and writing).

Lesson One: "The Politics of Recognition" Is Not a Thing

The problem is that institutional multiculturalism, like capitalist realism, actually does the opposite: it fatally limits our political imagination. This is true even when it means well. The way that Fanon himself has been appropriated by institutional multiculturalism

3   Fanon, *Black Skin, White Masks*, p. xi.

is a perfect example of how the call to decolonize the world—which is the call to imagine the world "changed inside out"—gets shrunk down to fit the world as it currently exists.

Charles Taylor's 1992 essay "The Politics of Recognition" is a key text for institutional multiculturalism; indeed, after Taylor first presented it as a lecture at Princeton, it was published, alongside a number of responses, in a book simply titled *Multiculturalism*. In his essay, Taylor, a scholar of European philosophy, pauses for a moment amidst a lengthy close reading of Hegel, Rousseau, and Kant, in order to consider Fanon's work. It doesn't take long—a bit less than two pages of a fifty-page essay—but it's enough space for Taylor to remove Fanon from the struggle for decolonization in order to re-introduce him as the main representative of multiculturalism, which for Taylor centers around "the demand for recognition."

It goes like this: according to Taylor, "*The Wretched of the Earth* argued that the major weapon of the colonizers was the imposition of their image of the colonized on the subjugated people. These latter, in order to be free, must first of all purge themselves of these depreciating self-images." (Taylor's entire reading of *The Wretched of the Earth* happens in those two sentences.) The main

struggle, then, is for "a changed self-image," fought
largely in university humanities departments (drumroll:
the canon wars!). The lesson of multiculturalism, simply put, "is that recognition forges identity, particularly
in its Fanonist application." "The struggle for freedom
and equality," Taylor concludes, "must therefore pass
through a revision of these images. Multicultural curricula are meant to help in this process of revision."[4]

Where Taylor winds up—with the idea that perhaps "a greater place ought to be made for women, and
for people of non-European races and cultures" in the
Western canon—is, I guess, preferable to the violence of
"monoculturalism." But as a reading of Fanon, it's just
insulting. Having spent much of his life treating the literal wounds of those victimized by the very real horrors
of colonization, Fanon knew all too well that the "major
weapon" of the colonizers was not "the imposition of
their image"; it was actual weaponry. Colonialism, he
wrote, is "not a machine capable of thinking, a body
endowed with reason," but simply "naked violence."[5]
But Taylor's Fanon, who wants nothing more than

4   Charles Taylor, "The Politics of Identity," in *Multiculturalism:
     Examining the Politics of Recognition*, ed. Amy Gutman (Princeton:
     Princeton University Press, 1994), p. 65-66.

5   Fanon, *Wretched of the Earth*, p. 23.

recognition, is the one that institutional multicultur-alism wants and needs. The best that currently exist-ing multiculturalism can offer is "a greater place" at the existing table. And austerity being what it is, there's much less on that table to go around today than there was back in the 1990s.

Decolonization isn't about a place at the table; it's about overturning the table altogether.

Lesson Two: The End of the World Is Already Here

As I've been insisting all along, it didn't have to turn out this way. We might as well start by reclaiming Fanon for our decolonized multiculturalism, from a figure asking "please sir may I have some recognition" to the one who calls us to the true task of decolonization: the end of the existing world. That's no doubt what he recognized in the lines from his teacher, Aimé Césaire, who reminds us that if our ultimate goal is decolonization, then "the only thing in the world worth starting" is "the end of the world."

Speaking of which: I have some bad news and some good news. The bad news first: it has gotten much easier to imagine the end of the world. In fact, we now have mul-tiple names for the end that seems each day to be getting closer: global warming, climate crisis, the Anthropocene. Deadly hurricanes and tornadoes, hell-on-earth fires, mudslides and avalanches, globe-encircling pandemics locking down whole nations at a time, millions victimized by famine and forced migration: and that's just the past three years. The world, as I write these sentences here at the end of the sci-fi sounding year of 2022, is looking properly apocalyptic.

Today's young activists, inheritors of the legacy of those who fought for a decolonized university and a decolonized world decades ago, found themselves arriving at birth upon a planet already marked by the certainty of irreversible climate change. For anyone doing politics today, there's no choice but to take Césaire's advice: the end of the world, in effect, is already here. As the by now well-worn saying goes, it's easier to imagine the end of the world than the end of capitalism. That's been true for quite a while now. Mark Fisher used that phrase a decade ago for the opening chapter of his book *Capitalist Realism*, and indeed, Fisher's main argument is that the daily functioning of capitalism—using the earth as raw material in order to accumulate more wealth—logically and inevitably leads to the end of the world.

That's the horror of capitalist realism: at the same time as it makes it harder and harder to imagine a "realistic" alternative to itself, it is slowly but inexorably carrying us to the end of the world, like a bus driver calmly driving off a cliff while reassuring the passengers that this really is the only way to get there. As Fisher's friend and comrade Jodi Dean put it in a lecture honoring his memory, simply put, capitalism *is* the end of the world.[6]

So the bad news is that it has gotten much easier to imagine the end of the world. Now for the good news: it has gotten much easier to imagine the end of the world. Please understand: I'm not making a joke here. I'm trying to take seriously the call of decolonization: to put an end to *this* world—precisely because the proper names for the end of the world we're currently living through are colonialism, capitalism, nationalism, heteropatriarchy, and racism.

We need to say these names. The usual narrative about climate change is that of a "natural disaster." And anyone who has watched a natural-disaster-themed movie can tell you that the lesson of such narratives is always the same: "We're all in this together!" But when it comes to the climate apocalypse, as Ajay Singh Chaudhary notes in the title of a recent article, "We're Not in This Together." Furthermore, there's nothing

6   Jodi Dean, "Capitalism Is the End of the World," *Mediations* 33.1-2 (2019).

"natural" about the climate crisis. Chaudhary tells us a much more disturbing story, one in which the proponents of business as usual know exactly where that business is leading us: towards a "3–5 degree Celsius change by the end of the twenty-first century." This is an outcome whose effects would include "mass levels of direct and indirect death, rampant disease in some regions, billions experiencing food and water insecurity, vast numbers of climate refugees, resource conflict, and so on."[7]

That may strike you, dear reader, as a horrifying outcome, but from an elite business-as-usual perspective, it all sounds relatively ok, or at least acceptable. Those currently benefitting from Actually Existing Capitalism would, under such circumstances, continue to benefit, and those who are already suffering would be the ones to keep suffering, or simply die off. Meanwhile, those at the top will double down on their current way of life, best described as an "armed lifeboat": protected and served by private security services and private firefighters, with privatized access to food and water and privatized education and medical services—in short, safe

7 Ajay Singh Chaudhary, "We're Not in This Together," *The Baffler* 51 (April 2020).

and sound and getting richer far above sea level while the world ends for the many.[8]

Most chilling of all, that future is already here. Scientific models suggest that based on current rates, by 2030, six million people could die each year from climate change. "This is a shocking number," Chaudhary notes, then hits us with an even more terrible shock: "the same models note that the world *currently* experiences some 4.5 million climate deaths per year." The difference between that seemingly apocalyptic outcome and our current reality, in other words, is ultimately just a statistical uptick in the current state of misery for much of the world.

The usual understanding of our political context is that right-wingers are uniformly climate change denialists, leaving frustrated liberals to scream: "Believe the science!" But many elite business-as-usual types are actually proponents of "right-wing climate realism," to use Chaudhary's phrase. They believe the science all right. But aboard their armed lifeboats, they're making their own calculations. From that particular vantage

8   The phrase "politics of the armed lifeboat" to describe the right-wing political response to climate change was coined by Christian Parenti in *Tropic of Chaos: Climate Change and the New Geography of Violence* (New York: Bold Type Books, 2012).

point, "simultaneously extending the life of our current global socioeconomic and political systems as long as possible for maximum real accumulation while 'cashing out' toward more directly coercive forms of privatized rule" makes total sense. Stay the course, present arms, full speed ahead!

"The end of the world," in other words, won't be an ending for everyone. If we keep to our present itinerary, some will do just fine, while others will drop dead. If you want a preview of how this will look, the COVID-19 pandemic provides a glimpse of what's to come.

Lesson Three: Imagine a Different Ending, Then Make It So

Wait, wasn't this supposed to be the good news? It is, but we've got to do some work to make it so. Chaudhary emphasizes that he's not trying to paint some inevitably dystopian picture of the future. Looking closely at what we call "the end of the world," he shows us that far from being a natural disaster, it's the result of good old human-made politics. More specifically, he unmasks the real villain: our old enemy, colonialism.

When we view the problem internationally, there's nothing all that new about today's end of the world via climate change. The Bengal famine of 1770 killed

10 million people—a third of the population of Bengal. As Mike Davis showed in his book *Late Victorian Holocausts*, this had nothing to do with "nature" and everything to do with the imposition of British colonialism. Or rather, colonialism, in the form of the British East India Company, ruthlessly fucked with nature: "new forms of capitalist imperialism transformed cyclical events like El Niño into 'natural' disasters. The famine was not the result of the ecological cycles but rather of the metabolic relation between a host of company policies, especially grain export, and the ecological system."[9] The same goes for "natural" disasters caused by colonial rule during the nineteenth and twentieth centuries in Algeria, Egypt, Angola, Queensland, Fiji, Samoa, and Haiti.

That's where the work of political imagination comes in. There is literally no one reading this book who isn't aware of the fact that at this very moment, millions of people are starving to death, in far-off places but also very likely within walking distance of where you are sitting right now. The question is: what do we do with that fact? What we do, mostly, is use neutral words like "poverty" or "famine" or "food insecurity"; mostly, we blame it on one or another "disaster." In 1943, there

9   Chaudhary, "We're Not in This Together."

was another Bengal Famine; "only" 4 million people died this time. The good and brave Winston Churchill explained that the "famine" was the result of population growth—Indians, he wrote, were "breeding like rabbits." "Overpopulation" indeed remains one of the most popular explanations for mass starvation. In fact, at the height of World War II, Churchill's colonial government was exporting massive amounts of grain from Bengal; colonialism was literally taking food out of the mouths of the colonized people of Bengal and leaving them to die. There was no "natural disaster" here; there was only what the economist Amartya Sen describes as "man-made famine."[10]

The proper name for all this is the one used by both Davis and Chaudhary: genocide. Another name for it is colonialism. That's why I agree so hard with Chaudhary's conclusion about the way to resist the right-wing climate realism that's leading us towards climate apocalypse: "the *politics of a left-wing climate realism* is a mode of broadened anti-colonial struggle, as much in the metropole as in the periphery." In other words, the proper name for a left-wing climate realism is decolonization.

10   Amartya Sen, *Poverty and Famines: An Essay on Entitlement and Deprivation* (Oxford: Clarendon Press, 1981).

Lesson Four: Decolonization Is Not *Not* a Cultural Event

We seem to have wandered pretty far from "multiculturalism" here. But that's only true if you stick to the script set up by Charles Taylor's "politics of recognition," or the administrators' austerity multiculturalism, or the diversity events offered by the Colorblind Rainbow Center for Campus Diversity. As I've been trying to convince you throughout this book, buried in the roots of today's institutional multiculturalism is the radical possibility that student movements fought for in the 1960s and 1970s. A different multiculturalism—*a decolonized version*—can also be a name for the reawakening of that buried but never defeated political imaginary.

Fanon would have nothing but scorn for Taylor's "politics of recognition," not to mention the idea that decolonization could happen via a reformed syllabus. What he called the "bare reality" of decolonization "reeks of red-hot cannonballs and bloody knives." Decolonization's "agenda of disorder," he adds, cannot be realized "if you are not determined from the very start to smash every obstacle encountered."[11]

11   Fanon, *Wretched of the Earth*, p. 3.

But Fanon also recognized that a key element of this quite literal fight for decolonization had to do with developing a decolonized political imagination. Indeed, the second half of *The Wretched of the Earth*—the part that folks like Taylor seem not to have gotten around to reading, which is why they tend to say things like "Fanon believes that violence is the solution"—focuses primarily on the importance of developing a decolonized national culture with an internationalist dimension. It's not that Fanon believes decolonization to be merely a cultural event, but it's also not *not* a cultural event. The relationship between the struggle for decolonization and the creation of a new, decolonized culture is therefore a dialectical one:

> the conscious, organized struggle undertaken by a colonized people in order to restore national sovereignty constitutes the greatest cultural manifestation that exists. It is not solely the success of the struggle that consequently validates and energizes culture; culture does not go into hibernation during the conflict. The development and internal progression of the actual struggle expand the number of directions in which culture can go and hint at new possibilities. . . . After the struggle is over, there is not only the demise of colonialism, but also the demise of the colonized.[12]

12   Fanon, *Wretched of the Earth*, p. 178.

That's a very different "end of the world" for us to imagine: the end of colonialism, and with it, the demise of the centuries-old world divided inexorably into colonized and colonizer.

Lesson Five: Live the Contradictions

So how do we get started on ending this world so we can begin a new one? And how is a decolonized multiculturalism going to help us get there?

This book began with a seeming contradiction: the fact that multiculturalism "won" the cultural wars of the 1980s and 1990s is a sign of the defeat of the radical movements of the 1960s and 1970s. That shiny Multicultural Center that claims to honor these movements might as well be their tombstone. These days, as Sara Ahmed teaches us, a document that documents the racism of the university can be used by that same university as proof of its commitment to "diversity." And this book itself, as I admitted in the preface, seems to be built on a contradiction: if decolonization is really "an agenda for total disorder," then how do you *organize* a political or educational project—not to mention a mass movement—around such an agenda?

Today, too much of what passes for politics begins and ends with simply pointing out contradictions; you tweet out the contradiction, shake your head piously at the hypocrisy of it all, and then move on. But Angela Davis, who was there fighting with decolonization movements in the 1960s and still is today, reminds us that contradictions are where our work *begins*. That's what dialectics is all about: "dialectics is based on discovering the contradictions in phenomena which can alone account for their existence. Reality is through and through permeated with contradictions. Without those contradictions, there would be no movement, no process, no activity."[13]

Davis' words are utterly crucial, but so too is the context in which she first spoke them. In 1969, having been fired from her job at UCLA by Governor Ronald Reagan for the crime of being a communist, Davis gave a series of public lectures for a course on "Recurring Philosophical Themes in Black Literature." By the time her notes were published as *Lectures on Liberation* in 1971, she was imprisoned and facing execution for the crime

13   Angela Y. Davis, *Lectures on Liberation* (New York: Committee to Free Angela Davis, 1971), p. 21-22. Rinaldo Walcott has also been exemplary in embodying the need to "live the contradictions" in order to do anti-racist/decolonizing work today. See Rinaldo Walcott, *The Long Emancipation: Moving toward Black Freedom* (Durham: Duke University Press, 2021); *On Property: Prisons, Policing, and the Call for Abolition* (Windsor: Biblioasis, 2021); and *Queer Returns: Essays on Multiculturalism, Diaspora and Black Studies* (Toronto: Insomniac Press, 2016).

of being Angela Davis. Struggles that begin in seminar rooms can spill out and find echoes in the streets, and vice versa. For Fanon, decolonization is, of course, fought for in the streets, but also at multiple other levels: in "individual encounters, a change of name for a sports club, the guest list at a cocktail party, members of a police force or the board of directors of a state or private bank," to name a few.[14] Dialectics applies everywhere to the struggle for liberation. As Fanon taught us and as Angela Davis continues to teach us, it calls to us from multiple sites, on multiple levels, simultaneously.

The End of the World, the Beginning of Decolonization

So let's be dialectical in concluding, in order to begin. Think of some of the stories I've told in this book. Look out across the landscape of the neoliberal university: diversity management, militarized tolerance, and austerity multiculturalism seem to be holding the ground as far as the eye can see. But dig a little deeper. "Diversity" wouldn't even be making an appearance on that horizon without the radical demands of the youth movements of the sixties and seventies: to open up the university, to wrench it from its settler colonial,

14   Fanon, *Wretched of the Earth*, p. 1.

white supremacist, and patriarchal capitalist origins, and to transform it into a place of radical democratic possibility. "Multiculturalism" wouldn't be a thing if these movements hadn't fought in the name of a radical internationalism—that is, in the name of decolonization. The campus police wouldn't need military-grade weaponry if these movements hadn't terrified the powerful so effectively. Austerity wouldn't have to be imposed so ruthlessly on public universities if they didn't represent sites at which the logic of capitalist realism stands in danger of being exposed as the fraud that it really is. And the power of resistance literature wouldn't have to be so carefully boxed in by "multicultural" syllabi if it didn't threaten to let loose the many political imaginaries of liberation.

Do we really want liberation, radical democracy, decolonization? If we do, then we need to see each of these "defeats" as temporary setbacks. We need to go back to the roots, and thence back to work. Remember: "At the level of description, decolonization is always a success." That involves an act of political imagination, in fact many such acts, one after the next. Once the struggle for decolonization is underway, everything looks different, because suddenly it can be described differently. With the coming of the struggle, the police siren and the military bugle, Fanon writes, no longer signify to the colonized: "Stay in your place!" but rather "Get ready to fight!" Decolonization requires smashing each obstacle encountered, so as we look out across our current landscape, we need the transformed vision that Fanon calls us to: "under certain circumstances an obstacle actually escalates action."[15] That's decolonization at its dialectical best.

I'm not saying imagination is enough; certainly, pretty words aren't. Some of this fight has to be crudely material in nature. For example, we need to fight on every possible front to save public education, which is currently being not simply underfunded but knowingly starved to death. We need public higher education to be funded so the university can be thrown open to those communities who have never been served by them or represented in them. We need more folks for the fight, and that means opening the gates. We need colleges and universities and all schools of any kind to be police-free zones, as a step towards the abolition of police everywhere.

I have some simple and concrete ideas about how to do some of this: tax the millionaires and billionaires; force the Ivies and other cushy private schools to cough up some of their bloated endowments to

15   Fanon, *Wretched of the Earth*, p. 16-17.

public institutions; find the administrators who receive $125,000 three-month consulting contracts to write reports about increasing diversity and then never write those reports and parade them through the streets, pelting them with tomatoes while forcing them to wear a sandwich-board sign that says "I Suck" (I would say send them to prison, but I'm an abolitionist).[16] I've got others; buy me a few beers and I'll tell you all about them. But without the necessary political imaginary to create the movements needed to realize such things, it's all just words.

Some fuel for that political imagination lies in the internationalist vision residing in multicultural literature: for example, the power to recapture lost moments of the past and open out onto possible moments in the future. This is the "past conditional temporality" described by

16   I wish this was hyperbole, but it's not: "A $125,000 contract with former University of Wisconsin System President Ray Cross required him to provide a 'written' report on how to increase diversity of students and staff at each UW campus, but nearly three months after his contract ended, no such written report exists . . . . UW Board of Regents President Drew Petersen assigned Cross to come up with recommendations. . .as part of a three-month consulting contract after his June 30 resignation. He was paid roughly $125,000 for work through Sept. 30." Kelly Meyerhofer, "UW's $125,000 Contract with Ray Cross Called for Written Report on Diversity, But He Never Wrote It," *La Crosse Tribune* (December 24, 2020).

Lisa Lowe in her book *The Intimacies of Four Continents*. "Reading literature," she writes, "is not a substitute for action, but a space for a different kind of thinking alongside it, an attention to both the 'what-could-have-been' and the 'what-will-be' that would otherwise be subsumed in the march of received official history." That in turn allows us to undertake what I have been calling on us to do throughout this book—return to the roots, in order to recapture from the past those possibilities that might have been and might still be in order to bring them into the future. It means developing a form of political imagination that makes it "possible to conceive the past, not as fixed or settled, not as inaugurating the temporality into which our present falls, but as a configuration of multiple contingent possibilities, all present, yet none inevitable."[17] The late great Palestinian poet Mourid Barghouti called this "triangular time (the past of moments, their present, and their future)."[18]

17   Lisa Lowe, *The Intimacy of Four Continents* (Durham: Duke University Press), 2015, p. 99, 175.

18   Mourid Barghouti, *I Saw Ramallah*, translated by Ahdaf Soueif (New York: Anchor Books, 2003), p. 43. A similar vision can be found in what Gary Wilder has recently and brilliantly called "concrete utopianism." See Gary Wilder, *Concrete Utopianism: The Politics of Temporality and Solidarity* (New York: Fordham University Press, 2022).

Fuel for the political imagination can be found, too, in the anti-racist visions that give rise to true models of diversity (without the management part). Paul Gilroy once told an interviewer that his writings over the past several decades have all been "marked by the desire to make it as easy for people to imagine a world without racial differences as it is for them currently to imagine the end of the world."[19] Indeed, here in 2022, it is in abolitionist movements that we can find the closest continuance of Fanon's description of the struggle for decolonization. Ruth Wilson Gilmore sums it up: "Abolition requires that we change just one thing: everything."[20] Working this through in a bit more detail, she describes the basis of abolition in a form that echoes what Fanon describes as decolonization:

> abolition has to be "green." It has to take seriously the problem of environmental harm, environmental racism, and environmental degradation. To be "green" it has to be "red." It has to figure out ways to generalize the resources needed for well-being for the most vulnerable people in our community, which then will extend to all people. And to do that,

19   Tommie Shelby, "Cosmopolitanism, Blackness, and Utopia: An Interview with Paul Gilroy," *Transition* 98 (2008).

20   See Ruth Wilson Gilmore, *Change Everything: Racial Capitalism and the Case for Abolition* (Chicago: Haymarket Books, 2023).

> to be "green" and "red," it has to be international. It
> has to stretch across borders so that we can consoli-
> date our strength, our experience, and our vision for
> a better world.[21]

Here then is a vision for the end of *this* world—one that
doesn't shy away from confronting the ongoing end of
the world via capitalist climate degradation—as well as
the beginning of another.

We must imagine a multiculturalism that truly represents this vision. That means leaning into the political
consequences of what happens when you bring together
cultures while holding to an internationalist perspective. Working backwards across Gilmore's list, we might
add that in order to be internationalist, a decolonized
multiculturalism needs to be red, and in order to be
red, it needs to be green. That also means starting from
the premise that doing multiculturalism means doing
politics—even (especially) when you're "just" reading
novels—because culture is political (and that's a good
thing). As Angela Davis wrote twenty-five years ago:
"A multiculturalism that does not acknowledge the
political character of culture will not, I am sure, lead

21   "Ruth Wilson Gilmore Makes the Case for Abolition,"
     Intercepted Podcast (June 10, 2020).

toward the dismantling of racist, sexist, homophobic, economically exploitative institutions."[22]

She was right, of course. And those long and difficult lists of things against which we commit ourselves to fight, lists that are constantly being changed and transformed as new identities and new forms of struggle arise, represent the landscape upon which a decolonized multiculturalism can open a space from which to carry on these cross-hatched fights. Institutional multiculturalism is, at best, the space in which "we" get to read about and culturally encounter "others" in order to learn the comforting lesson that we were all the same to begin with. A decolonized multiculturalism might instead become the space in which we (all of us) work through the revolutionary political concept developed by Black feminists in the Combahee River Collective and then amplified by thinkers like Kimberlé Williams Crenshaw and Patricia Hill Collins: *intersectionality*.

Addressing all the misinterpretations and misunderstandings and abuses of the term "intersectionality" would require a book in itself. But for our purposes, I have in mind Davis' conception: "not so much

22   Angela Y. Davis, "Gender, Class, and Multiculturalism: Rethinking 'Race' Politics," in Gordon and Newfield, *Mapping Multiculturalism*, p. 47.

intersectionality of identities, but intersectionality of struggles."[23] An awareness of and allegiance to this intersectionality of struggles—which she sees as key to forging transnational solidarities—involves attention to the *multiculturalism* inherent in both the most local and the most global levels:

> Our histories never unfold in isolation. We cannot truly tell what we consider to be our own histories without knowing the other stories. And often we discover that those other stories are actually our own stories. This is the admonition "Learn your sisters' stories" by Black feminist sociologist M. Jacqui Alexander. This is a dialectical process that requires us to constantly retell our stories, to revise them and retell them and relaunch them.[24]

Multiculturalism can and must become this dialectical process, this rethinking and revising and retelling and relaunching of our stories. And the struggle for decolonization means that in the process, not only our stories but "we" who tell them will be transformed.

That's the way this world ends, and a new one begins. Imagine that.

23 Angela Y. Davis, "Transnational Solidarities," in *Freedom Is a Constant Struggle: Ferguson, Palestine, and the Foundations of a Movement* (Chicago: Haymarket Books, 2016), p. 144.

24 Davis, "Transnational Solidarities," p. 134-35.

ACKNOWLEDGEMENTS

My first and most important thanks go to Bhakti Shringarpure, my editor (and friend and comrade), who read everything closely (and multiple times!), provided invaluable comments, pushed me when necessary and supported me when needed, and generally did all the things that a great editor is supposed to do but rarely does. There's no question that this is an infinitely better book than it would have been without her unsparing work.

A number of people were kind enough to have read and commented on the book while it was in progress, and I want to particularly thank members of the Committee on Globalization and Social Change seminar at the CUNY Graduate Center and my colleagues in the "Political Mobilizations and Social Movements" seminar at the Institute for Advanced Studies who read drafts of some of the sections and provided invaluable feedback. Tess Aldrich, Gary Wilder, Siraj Ahmed, Jesse Schwartz, Naomi Schiller, Anna Bernard, Patricia Alessandrini, and Debaditya Bhattacharya all offered important comments, criticism, and support at key moments. Libby Garland read much of this material before it was a book and saw what was of value (and what wasn't); her comments were crucial for guiding me through its later stages. Special thanks to Aslı Iğsız and Joan Scott, who read drafts with great generosity, even at moments of important disagreement, and to China Sajadian, who at a key moment in the writing process reminded me of the importance of making the post-9/11 context of repression (and especially the repression of the Palestine solidarity movement) part of the larger story of campus policing that I try to tell. Endless gratitude to Noura Erakat, Roderick Ferguson, and Daniel McNeil for their generous words. Big thanks to Emma Ingrisani and Colin Robinson and the crew at OR Books for their work in bringing this book into the world.

As for the larger debts that this book owes to the generations of writers, activists, and movements struggling for decolonization that have inspired me, I have tried to acknowledge my indebtedness in the Appendix. So I'll end by thanking Tess Aldrich and Mina Alessandrini for their unconditional love and support. I hope you guys like the book!

Decolonize Multiculturalism is dedicated to the student and youth movements of the past, present, and future. I hope it will be of some use in the struggle for a new world.

Brooklyn, February 2022

Appendix

RESOURCES FOR DECOLONIZERS

As I said at the outset, this book is really an attempt to bring together and build upon the important work done by generations of writers, activists, and movements struggling for decolonization—both of the university and of the world at large—for decades. So I wanted to include, here at the end, some suggestions for further reading, viewing, and doing, in hopes that readers will be inspired to keep going after reading this book. You can find full information about all the works listed here in the bibliography. So without further ado: have at it, decolonizers!

1. A Few Giants

Frantz Fanon: Frantz Fanon's book *The Wretched of the Earth*, published in 1961, has been described by Stuart Hall as "the bible of decolonization"; if you don't already have a copy, a sixtieth anniversary addition, with a new introduction by Cornel West, was just published. But to grasp the full development of Fanon's thinking about decolonization, as he pursued it throughout his short life (he died of leukemia at the age of 36, a few months after *The Wretched of the Earth* was published), it is worth reading his full body of work, from *Black Skin, White Masks* (published in 1954), to *A Dying Colonialism* (published in 1959), to the essays that were collected after his death as *Towards the African Revolution*. Happily, with the publication in English of the huge collection *Alienation and Freedom* in 2018, readers can now access much of Fanon's previously unavailable writings, including many of the articles that he published as part of his work as a psychiatrist, as well as two plays, which were never performed or published, that he wrote when he was young. For those wanting more, David Macey's biography of Fanon is truly excellent, if you are interested in reading more about his extraordinary life.

Angela Y. Davis: Let's just say it: Angela Y. Davis is the most important radical intellectual of our time. Hell, I would go further: she's the most important *intellectual* of our time, full stop. If you spend a minute looking around online, you'll find dozens of videos of her speaking—at academic conferences, at political demonstrations, at abolitionist meetings, and in all the public places where she has made important interventions over the course of six decades. But to get the full experience, you have to read her work. You might start with *The Angela Y. Davis Reader*, edited by Joy James, or with the book that has become the foundation of abolitionist thought, *Are Prisons Obsolete?* (2003). Or you could start with the two books with which she helped transform feminist studies—*Women, Race and Class* (1981) and *Women, Culture & Politics* (1990)—or the interviews collected in *Abolition Democracy* (2005) and *Freedom Is a Constant Struggle* (2015). For my money, though, you should start with *Lectures on Liberation*, published while she was a political prisoner: it collects several public lectures that she gave at UCLA in 1969 (after she had been fired by then-governor Ronald Reagan for being a Communist), and it is the most mind-blowing book I know. And six decades later, she has kept it going: *Abolition. Feminism. Now.*, a collaboration between Davis, Gina Dent, Erica R. Meiners, and Beth E. Richie, came out in 2022, and a new edition of *Angela Davis: An Autobiography* (first published in 1974, with Toni Morrison as the editor), with a new introduction by the author, was just published. Go get it.

Cedric J. Robinson: In Chapter Two, I tried to suggest how important the analysis provided by Cedric J. Robinson in his book *Black Marxism: The Making of the Black Radical Tradition* is for anyone interested in the struggle to decolonize the university. For many readers, *Black*

Marxism has literally been a life changer; just ask Robin
D. G. Kelley, who begins his preface to a new edition of
the book by saying as much: "I can say, without a trace
of hyperbole, that this book changed my life." First published in 1983 and re-issued in a new edition in 2000, the
influence of *Black Marxism* has been felt more and more
in the past decade, in particular through the power of
Robinson's analysis of *racial capitalism*, a key concept for
the intersectional struggle against capitalism and colonialism. But to grasp the full extent of Robinson's revolution, it's important to revisit his full body of work, from
his first book, *Terms of Order* (1980); to *Black Movements
in America* (1997) and *An Anthropology of Marxism* (2001),
which together serve as a sort of sequel to *Black Marxism*;
to *Forgeries of Memory and Meaning: Blacks and the Regimes
of Race in American Theater and Film Before World War II*
(2007), which brings together essays reflecting his life-
long interest in the relationship between representations
of race and the workings of racial capitalism. Cedric
J. Robinson passed away in 2016, but two recent vol-
umes (among many others) have helped carry his work
forward: *Cedric J. Robinson: On Racial Capitalism, Black
Internationalism, and Cultures of Resistance* (2019), which
brings together a number of Robinson's previously
uncollected articles (including his important work on

Black internationalism and anti-fascism), and *Futures of Black Radicalism* (2017), which includes work by contemporary scholar-activists inspired by and working to continue Robinson's radical legacy.

Ruth Wilson Gilmore: It's no coincidence that you'll find Ruth Wilson Gilmore's words quoted at the very beginning and the very end of this book. Her brilliant and unsparing work as a writer, scholar, teacher, and political organizer has been a radical inspiration to me, as it has for so many of us. Among other things, Gilmore has been crucial in advancing our understanding of and resistance to the Prison Industrial Complex—a phrase that has become part of many activists' vocabularies thanks to the organizing work done by Critical Resistance, the organization that Gilmore co-founded along with Angela Y. Davis and other scholar-activists in California in 1997. Her 2007 book *Golden Gulag: Prisons, Surplus, Crisis, and Opposition in Globalizing California* has been the single most important text for those wanting to understand the material and political underpinnings of the Prison Industrial Complex. *Golden Gulag* contains Gilmore's influential definition of racism—"the state-sanctioned and/or legal production and exploitation of group-differentiated vulnerabilities to premature death"—which has gained terrible resonance in the wake of the COVID-19 pandemic; together with her many subsequent articles and interventions, it has also helped to open up the work that she refers to as "abolition geography." Those wanting a starting point for engaging with her work might read Rachel Kushner's 2019 profile of Gilmore for the *New York Times Magazine*; or you could watch the short film *Geographies of Racial Capitalism with Ruth Wilson Gilmore*, produced by the Antipode Foundation, which you can find on YouTube; or you might start by listening to "Ruth Wilson Gilmore Makes the Case for Abolition," an interview that she did with Chenjerai Kumanyika for the "Intercepted" podcast in June 2020, which is an astonishing 90-minute master class on abolition. Finally, there are her two most recent books: *Abolition Geography: Essays Towards Liberation*, published in 2022, and *Change Everything: Racial Capitalism and the Case for Abolition*, forthcoming in 2023. Like all of her work over the course of a radical lifetime, they are gifts to those struggling towards liberation.

Roderick A. Ferguson: If I had to name one book that was the biggest inspiration for *Decolonize Multiculturalism*, it would be Roderick A. Ferguson's *We Demand:*

The University and Student Protests, published in 2017. *We Demand* is a brief and super readable account of how the student movements of the 1960s and 1970s, and their repressions by the state, corporations, and university administrators, have shaped the contemporary university. But what I admire about it most is that Ferguson has written it explicitly for a new generation of student activists, something I have also tried to do in this book. *We Demand* in many ways carries forward the more theoretical work that Ferguson had done in his 2012 book *The Reorder of Things: The University and Its Pedagogies of Minority Difference*, another crucial book for those wanting to understand how the contemporary university can unceasingly trumpet its commitment to diversity while simultaneously repressing minoritized communities. Ferguson's writing has also been exemplary for working at the intersection of race, gender, and sexuality, and in bringing together the energies of Black and queer liberation struggles: readers wanting to follow this thread should check out his first book, *Aberrations in Black: Toward a Queer of Color Critique* (2004) and his most recent one, *One-Dimensional Queer* (2019). Finally, he has co-edited two important books that should be on the shelves of all decolonizers: *Strange Affinities: The Gender and Sexual Politics of Comparative Racialization*, with Grace

Hong (2011) and *Keywords for African American Studies*, with Erica R. Edwards and Jeffrey O. G. Ogbar, which includes Nick Mitchell's scathing essay on "Diversity" as the "difference makes no difference."

Sara Ahmed: If you aren't a reader of Sara Ahmed's blog, Feminist Killjoys, you should be. In posts with provocative titles like "A Mess as a Queer Map," "Nodding as a Non-Performative," "Complaint as Feminist Pedagogy," "Apologies for Harm, Apologies as Harm," and "Queer Vandalism," you get to see Ahmed, a writer and scholar working at the intersection of feminist theory, queer theory, critical race theory, and postcolonial studies, thinking through devastatingly important ideas in real time (and, despite her self-identification as a "killjoy," she is a beautiful and very funny writer). As I noted in chapter five, Ahmed has been one of the keenest critics of the way that "diversity" has been institutionalized and depoliticized by universities, most incisively in her 2012 book *On Being Included: Racism and Diversity in Institutional Life.* Ultimately, her analysis of the depredations of academic institutions, and in particular the refusal of her own university to deal with systematic sexual harassment, led her to resign her academic position as Professor of Race and Cultural

Studies at the University of London, an act of deep integrity that she documented in several posts on Feminist Killjoys and has written about in her most recent books, *Living a Feminist Life* (2017) and *Complaint!* (2021). But long before that, she was focusing keenly on the ways that politics helps to determine the very nature of our being and frames our most intimate experiences, as a list of the titles of some of her many books indicates: *The Cultural Politics of Emotion* (2000), *Queer Phenomenology* (2006), *The Promise of Happiness* (2010), *Willful Subjects* (2014), and *What's the Use? On the Uses of Use* (2019).

2. The Short List

In addition to those giants of decolonization, here is a short reading list of crucial texts for those who want to go deeper into any of the issues raised in this book. They are arranged chronologically, and you can find full information about each of them in the bibliography.

- Toni Cade Bambara, "Realizing the Dream of a Black University" (1969)
- *The Combahee River Collective Statement* (1977)
- Edward W. Said, *Orientalism* (1979); *Culture and Imperialism* (1993)

- Cherríe Moraga and Gloria Anzaldúa, eds. *This Bridge Called My Back: Writings by Radical Women of Color* (1981)
- Ngũgĩ wa Thiong'o, *Decolonizing the Mind* (1986)
- Barbara Harlow, *Resistance Literature* (1987)
- Toni Morrison, "Unspeakable Things Unspoken: The Afro-American Presence in American Literature" (1990); *Playing in the Dark: Whiteness and the Literary Imagination* (1992)
- Hazel Carby, "The Multicultural Wars" (1992)
- Paul Gilroy, *The Black Atlantic* (1993); *Postcolonial Melancholia* (2006)
- David Theo Goldberg, *Multiculturalism: A Critical Reader* (1994)
- Avery F. Gordon and Christopher Newfield, *Mapping Multiculturalism* (1996)
- Robin D. G. Kelley, *Yo' Mama's Disfunktional! Fighting the Culture Wars in Urban America* (1997)
- Linda Tuhiwai Smith, *Decolonizing Methodologies: Research and Indigenous Peoples* (1999)
- Mark Fisher, *Capitalist Realism: Is There No Alternative?* (2009)
- Jodi Melamed, *Represent and Destroy: Rationalizing Violence in the New Racial Capitalism* (2011)

- Martha Biondi, *The Black Revolution on Campus* (2012)
- Stefano Harney and Fred Moten, *The Undercommons: Fugitive Planning & Black Study* (2013); *All Incomplete* (2021)
- Nora Barrows-Friedman, *In Our Power: U.S. Students Organize for Justice in Palestine* (2014)
- Strike Debt!, *The Debt Resisters' Operations Manual* (2014)
- Gurminder K. Bhambra, Dalia Gebrial, and Kerem Nişancıoğlu, eds., *Decolonising the University* (2018)
- Nick Mitchell, "Diversity" (2018)
- Eli Meyerhoff, *Beyond Education: Radical Studying for Another World* (2019)
- Debaditya Bhattacharya, *The Idea of the University: Histories and Contexts* (2018); *The University Unthought: Notes for a Future* (2019)
- Davarian L. Baldwin, *In the Shadow of the Ivory Tower: How Universities are Plundering Our Cities* (2021)
- Priyamvada Gopal, "On Decolonisation and the University" (2021)
- Anna Bernard, *Decolonizing Literature: An Introduction* (2023)

3. Join the Movement(s)

For those wanting next steps beyond further reading, below is a (very partial and incomplete) list of organizations, coalitions, and movement building spaces. The descriptions are taken from the groups themselves, and they are all of course easily findable on social media.

The Movement for Black Lives
m4bl.org

The Movement for Black Lives was created in 2014 as a space for Black organizations across the country to debate and discuss current political conditions; develop shared assessments of what political interventions were necessary in order to achieve key policy, cultural, and political wins; and convene organizational leadership in order to debate and co-create a shared movement-wide strategy. In 2016, The Movement for Black Lives launched the Vision for Black Lives, a comprehensive and visionary policy agenda.

Cops Off Campus Coalition
copsoffcampuscoalition.com

The Cops Off Campus Coalition is a network of local, regional, and transnational coalitions and collectives of students, educators, other workers, and all other community members impacted by police and policing at all levels of education. Guided by the transformative worldview of abolition, we work within our own communities and collectively to forward urgent alternatives to policing that will build a future University beyond punishment and violence.

Critical Resistance
criticalresistance.org

Critical Resistance seeks to build an international movement to end the Prison Industrial Complex (PIC) by challenging the belief that caging and controlling people makes us safe. We believe that basic necessities such as food, shelter, and freedom are what really make our communities secure. As such, our work is part of global struggles against inequality and powerlessness. The success of the movement requires that it reflect communities most affected by the PIC. Because we seek to abolish the PIC, we cannot support any work that extends its life or scope.

The Debt Collective
debtcollective.org

The Debt Collective is a membership-based union for debtors and our allies. It carries on the work of the Occupy movement and debt resister groups like Strike Debt! Our current economic system forces us into debt in various different areas of our lives: student debt for education; a mortgage to buy a home; debts for utility bills or phone bills, medical care, or even incarceration. No one should have to go into debt to meet their basic needs! These debts are illegitimate and the system needs to change, and we are united to win that change. How? Through the power of our union.

Palestine Legal
palestinelegal.org

Palestine Legal protects the civil and constitutional rights of people in the US who speak out for Palestinian freedom. Our mission is to bolster the Palestine solidarity movement by challenging efforts to threaten, harass, and legally bully activists into silence and inaction. We provide legal advice, Know Your Rights trainings, advocacy, and litigation support to college students, grassroots activists, and affected communities who stand for justice in Palestine. Palestine Legal also monitors incidents of suppression to expose trends in tactics to silence Palestine activism.

Decolonize This Place
decolonizethisplace.org

Decolonize This Place is an action-oriented movement and decolonial formation in New York City and beyond. It consists of grassroots groups and art collectives that seek to resist, unsettle, and reclaim the city. We aim to cultivate a politics of autonomy, solidarity, and mutual aid within a long-term, multi-generational horizon of decolonial, anti-capitalist, and feminist liberation.

CUNY for Palestine
linktr.ee/cuny4palestine

We are a diverse group of students, faculty, staff, and community members who organize at CUNY around Palestine solidarity, including supporting the Boycott, Divestment, and Sanctions movement and organizing with others towards Palestinian liberation.

Free CUNY!
linktr.ee/freecuny

We are a group of CUNY students, faculty, staff, and community members organizing to Free CUNY. We believe that free, high-quality, anti-racist higher education is a human right. In our vision, a Free CUNY is a liberating space.

BIBLIOGRAPHY

Adamson, Peter. "Arabic Translators Did Far More Than Just Preserve Greek Philosophy." *Aeon* (November 4, 2016).

—. *Philosophy in the Islamic World* (New York: Oxford University Press, 2016).

Adedoyin, Oyin. "Penn State Scraps Plans for a Racial-Justice Center." *Chronicle of Higher Education* (October 27, 2022).

Ahmad, Aijaz. *In Theory: Classes, Nations, Literatures* (New York: Verso, 1992), p. 98.

Ahmed, Sara. *Complaint!* (Duke University Press, 2021).

—. *The Cultural Politics of Emotion* (Edinburgh: Edinburgh University Press, 2000).

—. "Declarations of Whiteness: The Non-Performativity of Anti-Racism," *Borderlands* 3.2 (2004).

—. *Living a Feminist Life* (Duke University Press, 2017).

—. *On Being Included: Racism and Diversity in Institutional Life* (Durham: Duke University Press, 2012).

—. *The Promise of Happiness* (Durham: Duke University Press, 2010).

—. *Queer Phenomenology: Orientations, Objects, Others* (Durham: Duke University Press, 2006).

——. *What's the Use? On the Uses of Use* (Durham: Duke University Press, 2019).

——. *Willful Subjects* (Duke University Press, 2014).

Alessandrini, Anthony C. *Frantz Fanon and the Future of Cultural Politics: Finding Something Different* (Lanham, MD: Lexington Books, 2014).

——. "Our University: On Police Violence at CUNY." *Jadaliyya* (November 27, 2011).

——. "Palestine in Scare Quotes: From the NYT Grammar Book." *Jadaliyya* (July 12, 2011).

——. "TFW Your Former Colleague Turns Out to Be a Nazi." *Academe Blog* (December 9, 2019).

Alexander, Michelle. *The New Jim Crow: Mass Incarceration in the Age of Colorblindness* (New York: New Press, 2010).

Asaro, Salvatore. "Campus Unrest Part I: Queens College in the Spring of 1969" (November 5, 2018, available online).

Atwood, Margaret. "Headscarves to Die For." *The New York Times Book Review* (August 15, 2004).

Baldwin, Davarian L. *In the Shadow of the Ivory Tower: How Universities are Plundering Our Cities* (New York: Bold Type Books, 2021).

Bambara, Toni Cade. *"Realizing the Dream of a Black University" & Other Writings*, ed. Makeba Lavan and Conor Tomás Reed (CUNY Poetics Lost and Found, Series 7, Number 2, Fall 2017).

Barghouti, Mourid. *I Saw Ramallah*, translated by Ahdaf Soueif (New York: Anchor Books, 2003).

Barrows-Friedman, Nora. *In Our Power: U.S. Students Organize for Justice in Palestine* (Washington, DC: Just World Books, 2014).

Bass, Jack and Jack Nelson. *The Orangeburg Massacre* (Macon, GA: Mercer University Press, 1996).

Bauman, Dan. "Colleges Have Shed a Tenth of Their Employees Since the Pandemic Began." *Chronicle of Higher Education* (November 10, 2020).

Beecroft, Alexander. *An Ecology of World Literature: From Antiquity to the Present Day* (New York: Verso, 2015).

Bennett, William. *To Reclaim a Legacy: A Report on the Humanities in Higher Education* (Washington, DC: National Endowment for the Humanities [NEH], 1984).

Berlant, Lauren. "Trump, or Political Emotions." *The New Inquiry* (August 5, 2016).

Bernard, Anna. *Decolonizing Literature: An Introduction* (Cambridge: Polity Press, 2023).

Bhambra, Gurminder K., Dalia Gebrial, and Kerem Nişancıoğlu, eds. *Decolonising the University* (London: Pluto, 2018).

Bhattacharya, Debaditya, ed. *The Idea of the University: Histories and Contexts* (New York: Routledge, 2019).

——. *The University Unthought: Notes for a Future* (New York: Routledge, 2018).

Biondi, Martha. *The Black Revolution on Campus* (Berkeley: University of California Press, 2012).

——. "'Brooklyn College Belongs to Us': Black Students and the Transformation of Public Higher

Education in New York City," in Clarence Thomas, ed., *Civil Rights in New York City* (New York: Fordham University Press, 2011)

Blaise, Clark. "A Novel of India's Coming of Age." *New York Times Book Review* (April 19, 1981).

Bloom, Harold. *The Western Canon: The Books and School of the Ages* (New York: Harcourt Brace, 1994).

Blyth, Mark. *Austerity: The History of a Dangerous Idea* (New York: Oxford University Press, 2013).

Bond, Sarah E. "Whitewashing Ancient Statues: Whiteness, Racism and Color in the Ancient World." *Forbes* (April 27, 2017).

——. "Why We Need to Start Seeing the Classical World in Color." *Hyperallergic* (June 7, 2017).

Bossé, Haley, William Ren, darien k n manning, Claudia Inglessis, Louisa Belk, Michael Nettesheim, and Sareena Khanal. "Why We Left the Davis Center: Systemic Neglect and Structural Changes." *The Williams Record* (February 26, 2020).

Boyagoda, Randy. "Identity Crisis." *The Walrus* (July 2005).

Brown, Wendy. *In the Ruins of Neoliberalism: The Rise of Antidemocratic Politics in the West* (New York: Columbia University Press, 2019)

Bryson, Bethany. *Making Multiculturalism: Boundaries and Meaning in U.S. English Departments* (Palo Alto: Stanford University Press, 2005).

Butt, Tahir H. "'You Are Running a de Facto Segregated University': Racial Segregation and the City University of New York, 1961-1968," in *The Strange Careers of* the Jim Crow North: Segregation and Struggle outside of the South, ed. Brian Purnell and Jeanne Theoharis in collaboration with Komozi Woodard (New York: New York University Press, 2019).

Cainkar, Louise. "Targeting Muslims, at Ashcroft's Discretion." *Middle East Report Online* (March 14, 2003).

Carby, Hazel. *Cultures in Babylon: Black Britain and African America* (New York: Verso, 1999).

——. "The Multicultural Wars." *Radical History Review* 54.7 (1992).

Césaire, Aimé. *Notebook of a Return to My Native Land*, translated by Mireille Rosello with Annie Pritchard (New York: Bloodaxe, 1995.

Chamberlin, Victoria. "As Federal Programs Continue to Militarize Campus Cops, Some Universities Reconsider." *Guns & America* (July 9, 2020).

Chapman, Ben. "Thousands of CUNY Students Experience Homelessness and Food Insecurity, Report Says." *New York Daily News* (27 March 2019).

Chaudhary, Ajay Singh. "We're Not in This Together." *The Baffler* 51 (April 2020).

Clements, Jeffrey. "The Real History of 'Corporate Personhood': Meet the Man to Blame for Corporations Having More Rights Than You," *Alternet* (December 6, 2011).

"College Students Are More Diverse Than Ever. Faculty and Administrators Are Not." *AAC&U News* (March 2019).

The Combahee River Collective Statement: Black Feminist Organizing in the Seventies and Eighties (Albany, NY: Kitchen Table: Women of Color Press, 1986).

Cooper, Afua, Rinaldo Walcott and Lekeisha Hughes. "Robin D. G. Kelley and Fred Moten in Conversation." *Critical Ethnic Studies* 4.1 (2018).

Çubukçu, Ayça. *For the Love of Humanity: The World Tribunal on Iraq* (Philadelphia: University of Pennsylvania Press, 2018).

Davis, Angela Y. *Abolition Democracy: Beyond Empire, Prisons, and Torture* (New York: Seven Stories Press, 2005).

——. *Angela Davis: An Autobiography*, revised edition (Chicago: Haymarket Books, 2022).

——. *Are Prisons Obsolete?* (New York: Seven Stories Press, 2003).

——. *Freedom Is a Constant Struggle: Ferguson, Palestine, and the Foundations of a Movement* (Chicago: Haymarket Books, 2015).

——. "Gender, Class, and Multiculturalism: Rethinking 'Race' Politics," in Gordon and Newfield, *Mapping Multiculturalism*.

——. *Lectures on Liberation* (New York: Committee to Free Angela Davis, 1971).

——. *Women, Culture & Politics* (New York: Vintage, 1990).

——. *Women, Race and Class* (New York: Random House, 1981).

Davis, Angela, Gina Dent, Erica R. Meiners, and Beth E. Richie. *Abolition. Feminism. Now.* (Chicago: Haymarket Books, 2022).

Davis, Mike. *Late Victorian Holocausts: El Niño Famines and the Making of the Third World* (New York: Verso, 2002).

Dean, Jodi. "Capitalism Is the End of the World." *Mediations* 33.1-2 (2019).

Deparle, Jason. "Daring Research or 'Social Science Pornography'?: Charles Murray." *The New York Times Magazine* (October 9, 1994).

DeVega, Chauncey. "Alt-Right Catches Knight Fever—But Medieval Scholars Strike Back." *Salon* (November 30, 2017).

Dillin, John. "Conservative Republicans Call for 'Culture War,'" *Christian Science Monitor* (May 17, 1993).

Duggan, Lisa and Nan D. Hunter, *Sex Wars: Sexual Dissent and Political Culture* (New York: Routledge, 1995).

Eszterhas, Joe and Michael D. Roberts. *Thirteen Seconds: Confrontation at Kent State* (Cleveland: Gray & Company, 1970).

Fabricant, Michael and Stephen Brier. *Austerity Blues: Fighting for the Soul of Public Higher Education* (Baltimore: Johns Hopkins University Press, 2016).

Faircloth, Ryan. "University of Minnesota Deploys Safety Measures to Quell Crime Near Campus." *Minnesota Star Tribune* (September 10, 2021).

Fanon, Frantz. *Alienation and Freedom*, edited by Jean Khalifa and Robert J. C. Young, translated by Steven Corocan (New York: Bloomsbury Academic, 2018).

——. *Black Skin, White Masks*, translated by Richard Philcox (New York: Grove, 2008).

——. *A Dying Colonialism*, translated by Haakon Chevalier (New York: Grove, 1994).

——. *Toward the African Revolution*, translated by Haakon Chevalier (New York: Grove, 1994).

——. *The Wretched of the Earth*, translated by Richard Philcox (New York: Grove, 2004).

Feeney, Mark. "Orhan Pamuk Sees the World: The Turkish Writer's Work Serves as a Literary Bridge Between East and West." *Boston Globe* (October 11, 2004).

Ferguson, Roderick A. *Aberrations in Black: Toward a Queer of Color Critique* (Minneapolis: University of Minnesota Press, 2004).

——. *One-Dimensional Queer* (New York: Polity, 2019).

——. *The Reorder of Things: The University and Its Pedagogies of Minority Difference* (Minneapolis: University of Minnesota Press, 2012).

——. *We Demand: The University and Student Protests* (Berkeley: University of California Press, 2017).

Ferguson, Roderick A., and Grace Hong. *Strange Affinities: The Gender and Sexual Politics of Comparative Racialization* (Durham: Duke University Press, 2011).

Fisher, Alyssa. "What Is Identity Evropa?" *The Forward* (March 14, 2019).

Fisher, Mark. *Capitalist Realism: Is There No Alternative?* (London Zer0 Books, 2009).

Flaherty, Colleen. "Threats for What She Didn't Say." *Inside Higher Education* (June 19, 2017).

"Forces Fight Dawn-Dusk Battle for New College," *New York Amsterdam News* (March 7, 1964).

Foucault, Michel. "Preface," in Gilles Deleuze and Felix Guattari, *Anti-Oedipus: Capitalism and Schizophrenia*, trans. Robert Hurley, Mark Seem, and Helen R. Land (Minneapolis: University of Minnesota Press, 1983).

Gilmore, Ruth Wilson. "Abolition Geography and the Problem of Innocence," in *Futures of Black Radicalism*, ed. Gaye Theresa Johnson and Alex Lubin (New York: Verso, 2017).

——. *Abolition Geography: Essays Towards Liberation* (New York: Verso, 2022).

——. *Change Everything: Racial Capitalism and the Case for Abolition* (Chicago: Haymarket Books, 2023).

——. "Forgotten Places and the Seeds of Grassroots Planning," in *Engaging Contradictions: Theory, Politics, and Methods of Activist Scholarship* (Berkeley: University of California Press, 2008).

——. *Golden Gulag: Prisons, Surplus, Crisis, and Opposition in Globalizing California* (Berkeley: University of California Press, 2007).

——. "In the Shadow of the State," in *The Revolution Will Not Be Funded: Beyond the Non-Profit Industrial Complex*, ed. INCITE! Women of Color Against Violence (Durham: Duke University Press, 2017).

——. "The Worrying State of the Anti-Prison Movement." *Social Justice: A Journal of Crime, Conflict & World Order* (February 23, 2015).

Gilroy, Paul. *The Black Atlantic* (Cambridge: Harvard University Press, 1993).

——. *Postcolonial Melancholia* (New York: Columbia University Press, 2006).

Glazer, Nathan. *We Are All Multiculturalists Now* (Cambridge: Harvard University Press, 1998).

Glickman, Lawrence B. "Business as Usual: The Long History of Corporate Personhood." *Boston Review* (August 23, 2017)

Gluckman, Nell. "Why Did a University Suspend Its Mandatory Diversity Course?" *Chronicle of Higher Education* (March 18, 2021).

Goldberg, David Theo, ed. *Multiculturalism: A Critical Reader* (Cambridge: Blackwell, 1994).

Goldstein, Alexis. "Palestinians and Ferguson Protesters Link Arms Via Social Media." *Yes! Magazine* (August 16, 2014).

Gopal, Priyamvada. "On Decolonisation and the University." *Textual Practice* 35.6 (2021).

Gordon, Avery F. "The Work of Corporate Culture: Diversity Management," *Social Text* 44 (1995).

Gordon, Avery F. and Christopher Newfield, eds. *Mapping Multiculturalism* (Minneapolis: University of Minnesota Press, 1996).

Gounardes, Andrew and Timothy Hunter. "The Right to a Free and Quality Higher Education in New York." *Gotham Gazette* (November 26, 2019).

Grace, Thomas M. *Kent State: Death and Dissent in the Long Sixties* (Amherst: University of Massachusetts Press, 2016).

Green, Alex V. "The Emptiness and Inertia of 'Having Conversations.'" *Jezebel* (July 22, 2020).

Guerrero, M. Annette Jaimes. "Academic Apartheid: American Indian Studies and 'Multiculturalism,'" in Gordon and Newfield, *Mapping Multiculturalism*.

Gunderson, Christopher. "The Struggle for CUNY: A History of the CUNY Student Movement, 1969-1999" (available online).

Guzmán, María Constanza. *Gregory Rabassa's Latin American Literature: A Translator's Visible Legacy* (Lewisburg: Bucknell University Press. 2010).

Harlow, Barbara. *Resistance Literature* (New York: Methuen, 1987).

Harney, Stefano and Fred Moten. *The Undercommons: Fugitive Planning & Black Study* (New York: Minor Compositions, 2013).

——. *All Incomplete* (New York: Minor Compositions, 2021).

Hartman, Andrew. *A War for the Soul of America: A History of the Culture Wars* (Chicago: University of Chicago Press, 2015).

Harvey, David. *The Anti-Capitalist Chronicles* (London: Pluto Press, 2020).

——. *A Brief History of Neoliberalism* (New York: Oxford University Press, 2007).

Hass, Robert. "Poet-Bashing Police." *New York Times* (November 19, 2011).

Hegerfeldt, Anne C. *Lies that Tell the Truth: Magic Realism Seen through Contemporary Fiction from Britain* (Amsterdam: Rodopi, 2005).

Ignatiev, Noel. *How the Irish Became White* (New York: Routledge, 1994).

Jackson, Lauren Michele. "What Is an Anti-Racist Reading List For?" *Vulture* (June 4, 2020).

——. *White Negroes: When Cornrows Were in Vogue . . . and Other Thoughts on Cultural Appropriation* (Boston: Beacon Press, 2019).

Jaschik, Scott. "U of Chicago to Freshmen: Don't Expect Safe Spaces." *Inside Higher Ed* (August 25, 2016).

Johnson, Gaye Theresa, and Alex Lubin, eds. *Futures of Black Radicalism* (New York: Verso, 2017).

Joiner, Fred L. "Austerity." *Delaware Poetry Review* 8.1 (2016).

Jordison, Sam. "Orhan Pamuk's *Snow*: A Book About 'Other' People—and Therefore Us." *The Guardian* (March 20, 2018).

Kanafani, Ghassan. *Literature of Resistance in Occupied Palestine: 1948-1966* (Beirut: Institute for Arab Research, 1982).

Karaganis, Joe and David McClure. "Did Harold Bloom or Toni Morrison Win the Literary Canon Wars?" *The New York Times* (October 19, 2019).

Katzenstein, Jessica. *The Wars Are Here: How the United States' Post-9/11 Wars Helped Militarize U.S. Police*, "Costs of War" Project, Watson Institute for International and Public Affairs, Brown University (September 16, 2020).

Kelley, Robin D. G. *Yo' Mama's Disfunktional! Fighting the Culture Wars in Urban America* (Boston: Beacon Press, 1997).

Kennedy, Randall. *For Discrimination: Race, Affirmative Action, and the Law* (New York: Pantheon, 2013).

Kim, Dorothy. "Teaching Medieval Studies in a Time of White Supremacy." *In the Middle* (August 28, 2017).

Kim, Yunkyo and Megan Munce. "Students Call on University to Divest from Police Forces and Invest in Black Communities." *The Daily Northwestern* (June 10, 2020).

Kozol, Jonathan. *The Shame of the Nation: The Restoration of Apartheid Schooling in America* (New York: Random House, 2005).

——. "Still Separate, Still Unequal: America's Educational Apartheid," *Harper's* (September 2005).

Kushner, Rachel. "Is Prison Necessary? Ruth Wilson Gilmore Might Change Your Mind." *The New York Times Magazine* (April 17, 2019).

Kymlica, Will. *Multicultural Citizenship: A Liberal Theory of Minority Rights* (Oxford: Clarendon Press, 1996).

Lane, Anthony. "*Eurovision Song Contest: The Story of Fire Saga.*" *New Yorker* (June 6 & 13, 2020).

Lewis, Anthony. "A Solomonic Decision." *The New York Times* (June 29, 1978).

Lopez, German. "Samuel DuBose: What We Know About the University of Cincinnati Police Shooting." *Vox* (July 30, 2015).

Lowe, Lisa. *The Intimacy of Four Continents* (Durham: Duke University Press, 2015).

Luckett, Robert. "Why the Jackson State Massacre Still Matters." *The New York Times* (May 14, 2020).

Macey, David. *Frantz Fanon: A Life* (New York: Picador, 2000).

Meyerhofer, Kelly. "UW's $125,000 Contract with Ray Cross Called for Written Report on Diversity, But He Never Wrote It." *La Crosse Tribune* (December 24, 2020).

Meyerhoff, Eli. *Beyond Education: Radical Studying for Another World* (Minneapolis: University of Minnesota Press, 2019).

McKenzie, Lindsay. "Words Matter for College Presidents, but So Will Actions." *Inside Higher Education* (June 8, 2020).

McNeil, Daniel. "Even Canadians Find It a Bit Boring: A Report on the Banality of Multiculturalism, Immigration and Race Relations." *Canadian Journal of Communication* 46.3 (2021).

——. *Thinking While Black: Translating the Politics and Popular Culture of a Rebel Generation* (New Brunswick: Rutgers University Press, 2022).

——. "Wrestling with Multicultural Snake Oil: A Newcomer's Introduction to Black Canada." *Unsettling the Great White North: Black Canadian History*, eds. Michele A. Johnson and Funké Aladejebi (Toronto: University of Toronto Press, 2021).

Melamed, Jodi. *Represent and Destroy: Rationalizing Violence in the New Racial Capitalism* (Minneapolis: University of Minnesota Press, 2011).

McInnis, Tatiana and Amanda Lehr. "The Colorblind Rainbow Center for Campus Diversity Seeks a

New Director to Tell Us That Nothing Is Wrong."
McSweeney's Internet Tendency (July 8, 2020).

Mitchell, Nick. "Diversity," in *Keywords for African American Studies*, ed. Erica R. Edwards, Roderick A.

Ferguson, and Jeffrey O. G. Ogbar (New York: New York University Press, 2018).

Moraga, Cherríe, and Gloria Anzaldúa, eds. *This Bridge Called My Back: Writings by Radical Women of Color* (New York: Kitchen Table/Women of Color Press, 1983).

Morrison, Joan and Robert K. Morrison, eds. *From Camelot to Kent State: The Sixties Experience in the Words of Those Who Lived It* (New York: Times Books, 1987).

Morrison, Toni. *Playing in the Dark: Whiteness and the Literary Imagination* (Cambridge: Harvard University Press, 1992).

—. "Unspeakable Things Unspoken: The Afro-American Presence in American Literature," *Tanner Lectures on Human Values, XI* (Salt Lake City: University of Utah Press, 1990), p. 132.

Murch, Donna Jean. *Living for the City: Migration, Education, and the Rise of the Black Panther Party in Oakland, California*. Chapel Hill: University of North Carolina Press, 2010.

Nelson, Libby. "Why Nearly All Colleges Have an Armed Police Force." *Vox* (July 29, 2015).

Ngũgĩ wa Thiong'o. *Decolonizing the Mind* (Portsmouth, NH: Heinemann, 1986).

—. "Literature in Schools," in *Writers in Politics* (London: Heinemann, 1981).

——. "On the Abolition of the English Department," in *Homecoming: Essays* (London: Heinemann, 1972).

Offenhartz, Jake. "NYC Psychology Professor Secretly Moonlights as White Nationalist Co-Host of Richard Spencer's Podcast." *Gothamist* (November 8, 2019).

"On Neoliberalism: An Interview with David Harvey," *Monthly Review* (June 19, 2006).

Onion, Rebecca. "The Woman Who Wanted *Beloved* Banned from Schools Is Right About One Thing." *Slate* (October 31, 2021).

Otterman, Sharon. "Black Columbia Student's Confrontation with Security Becomes Flashpoint Over Racism on Campus." *The New York Times* (April 18, 2019).

The Palestine Exception to Free Speech: A Movement Under Attack in the US. (New York: Palestine Legal and the Center for Constitutional Rights, 2015).

Painter, Nell Irvin. *The History of White People* (New York: W. W. Norton, 2010).

Pamuk, Orhan. *Snow,* translated by Maureen Freely (New York: Vintage, 2005).

Parenti, Christian. *Tropic of Chaos: Climate Change and the New Geography of Violence* (New York: Bold Type Books, 2012).

Parini, Jay and Keegan Callanan et al. "Middlebury's Statement of Principle." *The Wall Street Journal* (March 6, 2017).

Parvini, Sarah. "UC Davis Spends $175,000 to Sanitize Its Online Image After Ugly Pepper Spray Incident." *Los Angeles Times* (April 14, 2016).

Patrick, Bob. "Diversity and Multiculturalism." *The Inclusive Latin Classroom* (May 5, 2019).

Patton, Laurie. "The Right Way to Protect Free Speech on Campus." *The Wall Street Journal* (June 10, 2017).

Peyser, Eve. "Biden Trashes Millennials in Quest to Become Even Less Likable." *Vice* (January 12, 2018).

Phillips, Amber. "Steve King: The Idea that Every Culture Is Equal Is 'Not Objectively True.'" *The Washington Post* (July 20, 2016).

Pierrot, Grégory. *Decolonize Hipsters* (New York: OR Books, 2020).

Piquant, Juvanie. "Imposing Tuition at CUNY Was Systemic Racism. This Year, We Can Fix It." *Gotham Gazette* (March 26, 2021).

Rani, Bhargav. "Revolution and CUNY: Remembering the 1969 Fight for Open Admissions." *GC Advocate* (30 July 2018)

Rattansi, Ali. *Multiculturalism: A Very Short Introduction* (New York: Oxford University Press, 2011).

The Report of the President's Commission on Campus Unrest (Washington, DC: U.S. Department of Health, Education, and Welfare, 1970).

Robbins, Bruce. *Feeling Global: Internationalism in Distress* (New York: New York University Press, 1999).

Robinson, Cedric J. *An Anthropology of Marxism* (Chapel Hill: University of North Carolina Press, 2019).

——. *Black Marxism: The Making of the Black Radical Tradition* (Chapel Hill: University of North Carolina Press, 2000).

——. *Black Movements in America*. New York: Routledge, 1997.

——. *Cedric J. Robinson: On Racial Capitalism, Black Internationalism, and Cultures of Resistance*, ed. H. L. T. Quan (New York: Pluto, 2019).

——. *Forgeries of Memory and Meaning: Blacks and the Regimes of Race in American Theater and Film Before World War II* (Chapel Hill: University of North Carolina Press, 2007).

——. "Manichaeism and Multiculturalism," in Gordon and Newfield, *Mapping Multiculturalism*.

——. "Ota Benga's Flight Through Geronimo's Eyes: Tales of Science and Multiculturalism," in Goldberg, *Multiculturalism*.

——. *Terms of Order: Political Science and the Myth of Leadership* (Albany: State University of New York Press, 1980).

Robinson, Kenton. "Foe to Those Who Would Shape Literature to Their Own Ends." *Harford Courant* (October 4, 1994).

Rodriguez, Dylan. "Reformism Isn't Liberation, It's Counterinsurgency." *Medium* (October 20, 2020).

Roediger, David. *The Wages of Whiteness: Race and the Making of the American Working Class* (New York: Verso, 1991).

Ronda, Michelle. "The Children of the Whole People Can Be Educated," in *Women on the Role of Public Higher Education: Personal Reflections from CUNY's Graduate Center*, ed. Deborah S. Gambs and Rose M. Kim (New York: Palgrave Macmillan, 2015).

Rushdie, Salman. *Imaginary Homelands: Essays and Criticism 1981-1991* (London: Granta, 1991).

——. *Midnight's Children: A Novel* (New York: Penguin, 1991).

"Ruth Wilson Gilmore Makes the Case for Abolition," *Intercepted Podcast* (June 10, 2020).

Said, Edward W. *Culture and Imperialism* (New York: Vintage, 1993).

——. *Humanism and Democratic Criticism* (New York: Columbia UP, 2004).

——. *Orientalism* (New York: Vintage, 1979).

Scott, David. *Omens of Adversity: Tragedy, Time, Memory, Justice* (Durham: Duke University Press, 2014).

Scott, James. *Weapons of the Weak: Everyday Forms of Peasant Resistance* (New Haven: Yale University Press, 1985).

Sen, Amartya. *Poverty and Famines: An Essay on Entitlement and Deprivation* (Oxford: Clarendon Press, 1981).

Serwer, Adam. "Why Conservatives Want to Cancel the 1619 Project." *The Atlantic* (May 21, 2021).

Shamas, Diala and Nermeen Arastu. *Mapping Muslims: NYPD Spying and Its Impact on American Muslims* (New York: Muslim American Civil Liberties Coalition (MACLC) and Creating Law Enforcement Accountability & Responsibility (CLEAR) Project, 2013).

Shelby, Tommie. "Cosmopolitanism, Blackness, and Utopia: An Interview with Paul Gilroy." *Transition* 98 (2008).

Shringarpure, Bhakti. "Decolonizing Education: A Conversation with Linda Tuhiwai Smith." *Los Angeles Review of Books* (May 18, 2021).

——. "Notes on Fake Decolonization." *Africa Is a Country* (December 18, 2020).

Sitze, Adam. "Academic Unfreedom, Unacademic Freedom." *The Massachusetts Review* 58.4 (2017).

Skelding, Conor. "CUNY: 'No Knowledge' of Undercover NYPD Targeting Muslims on Campus." *Politico* (November 24, 2015).

Speri, Alice. "Israel Security Forces Are Training American Cops Despite History of Rights Abuses." *The Intercept* (September 15, 2017).

Spivak, Gayatri Chakravorty. *Outside in the Teaching Machine* (New York: Routledge, 1993).

Stahl, Aviva. "Brooklyn College Students: NYPD Illegally Spied on Us and Lied About It." *Gothamist* (January 5, 2016).

——. "NYPD Undercover 'Converted' to Islam to Spy on Brooklyn College Students." *Gothamist* (October 29, 2015).

Steinberg, Shirley R., ed. *Diversity and Multiculturalism: A Reader* (New York: Peter Lang, 2009).

Stout, Cathryn and Gabrielle LaMarr LeMee. "Efforts to Restrict Teaching About Racism and Bias Have Multiplied Across the U.S." *Chalkbeat* (22 July 2021).

Strike Debt! *The Debt Resisters' Operations Manual* (New York: PM Press, 2014).

Taylor, Charles. "The Politics of Identity," in *Multiculturalism: Examining the Politics of Recognition*, ed. Amy Gutman (Princeton: Princeton University Press, 1994).

Taylor, Keeanga-Yamahtta. "Black Feminism and the
    Combahee River Collective." *Monthly Review*
    (January 1, 2019).

Theoharis, Jeanne. "'I Feel Like a Despised Insect': Coming
    of Age Under Surveillance in New York." *The Intercept*
    (February 18, 2016).

Theoharis, Jeanne, Alan Aja and Joseph Entin. "Spare
    CUNY, and Save the Education our Heroes Deserve."
    City Limits (May 13, 2020).

"Trump Administration Declares Multiculturalism Is 'Not
    Who America Is' as WH Releases Racist, Revisionist
    Report." *Democracy Now!* (20 January 2021).

Tyner, James A. and Mindy Farmer. *Cambodia and Kent
    State: In the Aftermath of Nixon's Expansion of the Vietnam
    War* (Kent, OH: Kent State University Press, 2020).

Tuck, Eve, and K. Wayne Yang. "Decolonization Is not
    a Metaphor." *Decolonization: Indigeneity, Education &
    Society* 1.1 (2012).

"Tucker Carlson: The Far-Left Agenda Your Children
    Are Being Taught Every Day," Fox News
    (February 19, 2021).

Tuhiwai Smith, Linda. *Decolonizing Methodologies: Research
    and Indigenous Peoples*, second edition (London: Zed
    Books, 2012).

Venuti, Lawrence. *The Translator's Invisibility: A History of
    Translation* (New York: Routledge, 1995).

Walcott, Rinaldo. *The Long Emancipation: Moving toward
    Black Freedom* (Durham: Duke University Press, 2021).

——. *On Property: Prisons, Policing, and the Call for Abolition* (Windsor: Biblioasis, 2021).

——. *Queer Returns: Essays on Multiculturalism, Diaspora and Black Studies* (Toronto: Insomniac Press, 2016).

Wavy the Bear. "Can the Managerial Technique Speak?" *Journal of Academic Freedom* 11 (2020).

Weiss, Philip. "They Up and Died!" *Mondoweiss* (October 14, 2010).

Weissman, Sara. "Over 100 Campus Police Departments Got Military Equipment Through This Federal Program." *Diverse: Issues in Higher Education* (July 20, 2020).

Wilder, Gary. *Concrete Utopianism: The Politics of Temporality and Solidarity* (New York: Fordham University Press, 2022).

Williams, Cobretti D. "Race and Policing in Higher Education." *The Activist History Review* (November 19, 2019).

Woodsworth, Michael. *Battle for Bed-Stuy: The Long War on Poverty in New York City* (Cambridge: Harvard University Press, 2016).

Wright, Angela. "How Armed Police Officers on Campus Have Become a Ubiquitous Part of American College Life." *MacLean's* (June 25, 2020).

CPSIA information can be obtained
at www.ICGtesting.com
Printed in the USA
JSHW021029050423
39886JS00001B/1